Orbital Progressions

A R-evolutionary Timing Technique

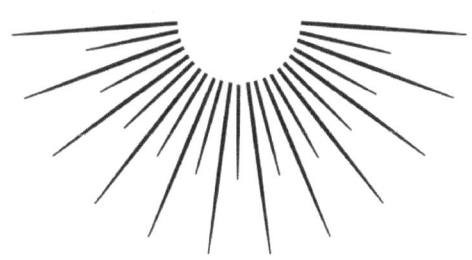

Mercy Joy Morales

Copyright © 2023 by Mercy Joy Morales

All rights are reserved

ISBN-13: 979-8-89184-988-4

Credit Chart images: Astro Gold

Table of Contents

Chapter 1: Evolving the Natal Chart with Progressions 1

Chapter 2: What exactly are Orbital Progressions? 7

Chapter 3: Astrologers 15

Chapter 4: Athletes with Dramatic Identity Shifts 36

Chapter 5: Authors 42

Chapter 6: Births 48

Chapter 7: Bitcoin 57

Chapter 8: Come Back Queens of Stranger Things 63

Chapter 9: Musicians 69

Chapter 10: Royals 78

Chapter 11: Saints 84

Chapter 12: Sage & Scientist 90

Chapter 13: The USA 96

Epilogue 99

Thank you to...

My loving husband, Jonathon, for his steady support through the highs, the lows, and the countless times he heard "make your own dinner".

My beautiful children, Mia, Carlos, Mason, Claire, and Zoe; and grandchildren, Hendi and Mayan Ra, for their encouragement and patience as I followed my passion.

The rest of my fabulous family for humoring my astrology musings, even when they didn't know what the f* I was talking about.

My friend and astrology mentor, Robert Brown, for our enlightening Thursday mornings and book review.

My brilliant soul sister, Justine Ligon, for her editorial expertise and advice.

OPA President, Kay Taylor, for her publishing suggestions and guidance.

All of the astrologers in this book, and outside of it, who have shared their insight and wisdom.

My faithful writing companions and trusty sidekicks, Olive, our 20-year-old dog, and Shadrach, the cat.

Chapter 1
• • • • • • • •
Evolving the Natal Chart with Progressions

Evolution happens. As the wheel of life turns, experiences shift our consciousness into a whole new way of perceiving the world around us. Most of us can look back and easily see that the person we were ten years ago is a much different version of who we are now.

How does astrology track this? Theoretically, we track it with a progressed chart. A progressed chart provides a wellspring of information. As our natal planets make their journey through our progressed chart, they reflect the energy of our life in the "now" moment, in relation to our natal chart.

There has been one main timing technique that has been utilized since the 17th century, Secondary Progressions. Placidus de Titus (born 1603) is credited with creating the method as it stands now; although, Vettius Valens (born 120 AD) mentions progressing the Sun by adding a day for each year. Johannes Kepler (born 1571) is noted to have used this with the Sun as well. Often within the mystery of history we simply don't have all of the information to determine an exact origin. So of course, we must always consider that the roots of this method may have sprouted from another culture.

In addition to Secondary Progressions, there are other types of progression techniques we use: Solar Arch, Tertiary, etcetera. They each offer a valid and interesting perspective. Orbital Progressions, the technique defined within this book, provides noteworthy data and insight that will enhance any astrologer's understanding of each chart you read. This method is not intended to disprove or be more accurate than other progression methods. It's simply a great addition to the astrological tool box.

In case you're not super familiar with what a progressed chart is, here are a few Cliff's Notes…

When we're looking at progressions, we have to first look at our natal chart; we must know where we've been to better understand where we are going. When we look at our natal chart, what we are looking at is a framework for the main program we are running for this incarnation.

As we know, the natal chart is a map of where the planets were in the sky at the moment you took your first breath. That energetic signature creates the infrastructure for this lifetime. From the first moment we are born, we start accumulating knowledge. The cosmos is always in motion, and so are we. As the planets move through the sky, they are revolving around our birth chart, transiting and eclipsing our natal planets, as well as our progressed planetary placements.

The information and experiences these transits deliver synchronistically propel our soul's evolution. Events can come hard and fast, but evolution tends to be a slower process. It takes time for us to digest, absorb, and process energies from these planetary transits. This is where our progressed chart powerfully comes into play. Progressions show where we are at in the advancement of our consciousness.

Of course, there's no end to the advancement of our consciousness. Eternal growth is the name of the game. So, there isn't any race to the finish line; no need to compare the journey of one with the journey of another. We are simply in the process of becoming more self-aware. The science of astrology allows us to more thoroughly comprehend our experience on planet Earth.

Progressions, in particular, are incredibly important to take note of when we are assessing a chart. They give you the most current data on yourself or your client, and are absolutely necessary in accurately predicting up-and-coming trends.

Imagine for a moment a traditional clock with a face.

The second hand is turning quickly, keeping track of shorter cycles.

This determines the rate of movement of the minute hand, which is turning more slowly than the second hand, keeping track of longer cycles.

This is precisely how progressions work. The transiting planets are moving more quickly, determining the slower rate of motion of the progressed planets. There is simultaneous action happening between the two cycles.

Spiritually, we are always leveling up, even when it looks like we are going backwards. As long as we're alive, we can't stop experiencing and therefore adding to the pot, so we are always expanding to become more. At differing moments in life profound shifts occur which add dimension to our fundamental nature. It's a layering effect. We'll see these mirrored by our progressed planets.

It's a bit like having a Mac OS. Let's say it's running the Monterey program. It's good, doing the necessary things. But then, here comes this new improved Ventura version that does all those things and more. It will provide an expanded capability in user experience, while still running it on the original Mac. We too have an original program blueprint, our birth chart, and we receive upgrades as we play the game of life.

As astrologers, when we use accurate timing techniques, our predictive ability strengthens. We all have our own method of how we prefer to use them. Some like to evaluate progressed charts, or other timing techniques, independently as if they are their own entity. There's really no getting it wrong. I personally always use them in tandem with the natal chart for the most holistic analysis.

With progressed planets we are taking the original planetary placement and adding a new dimension to it. Perhaps we can further understand it by equating it to musical notes. For example, let's say our natal Sun is the monad, middle C, resonating one powerful frequency.

The sign that the Sun is in has a ruling planet. For the sake of this conversation, we will say the Sun is in Virgo, ruled by Mercury, which we will assign the note E to.

These two, in a sense, are functioning as a dyad. This dual frequency will be resounding your whole life.

Now, if we add the note of your progressed, let's say, Scorpio Sun, note G, we are hearing/feeling/experiencing a triad of energy. C-E-G. The triad changes when the progressed Sun enters a new sign, adding a new vibrational layer.

F.Y.I. All the planetary notes that are playing at the time of your birth create your soul song, in hippie terms.

When we know what our progressed planets are doing, then we can fully embrace those energies and mine them for all they have to offer. That Virgo Sun person can really learn so much valuable information by now digging deeper into the Earth for answers instead of just harvesting what's growing on top of the surface. There's still the Virgo but it's got an additional Scorpionic influence.

Outside of an evolutionary perspective, progressions offer invaluable information whether we are looking at mundane, medical, financial astrology, etc. If we leave progressed analysis out of our readings, we run the risk of missing out on key timings, opportunities, and insight. When you're trying to catch a wave, you need to start paddling before the wave reaches you in order to stand up and ride it.

Mastering life is mastering timing. Subconsciously we know this. Ever heard the phrase, "Timing is everything."? As astrologers, we have the wherewithal to back up and view the big picture. This is where we are of great service to our clients. Like a conductor to an orchestra, we advise on when to take appropriate actions.

Does this mean our clients will always take that guidance? Or ourselves for that matter? Ha,ha… no, and that's ok. One of the amazing things about how the Universe operates is that opportunity will always present itself again, it will just be in another time and way.

Each planet in its progressed state has much to tell us. Sometimes progressions can be referred to as a "metaphorical representation" or an "artificial movement" of the planets through time; but, after my studies with Orbital Progressions, I rather lean towards progressions being a more literal and true representation, as real as each revolution Earth takes around the sun equals a year of life. It's a time measurement based on a mathematical formula, not a guess. When we see Orbital Progressions for what they are, mathematical evolution, then we can understand their potency.

There is much benefit to working with Orbital Progressions. As we look through the charts in this book, we may come to understand that while the symbology is there, so are the corporeal circumstances and events. The irrefutable proof lies within the alignments, no different than normal transits.

Chapter 2

What exactly are Orbital Progressions?

Good question. Orbital Progressions are a timing technique that takes into account the authentic rate of orbit of each planet.

The rate at which we progress the sun in a chart, one degree a year, is used as a constant across many progression methods, including this one. The reason being is, well, it works. A correlation exists between the Earth's rotation and the Earth's orbit There's a historical and general consensus that it accurately portrays the evolution of one's identity, and corresponds with the more mundane, and sometimes miraculous, occurrences of everyday life.

We progress the Sun at an average rate of 1 degree per year because it takes roughly that to orbit 360°. Based on this, wouldn't it make sense to progress the other planets by their averaged rates of rotation around the Sun? Orbital Progressions do just that. They are based on the average rate of movement.

When I first realized this technique, I was utterly fascinated. First, by its accuracy; I went over a plethora of charts and they all rang true to experience. Secondly, by the fact that two different techniques, Orbital Progressions / Secondary Progressions, could tell the same story so well, only through differing placements. They actually validate each other.

This anomaly isn't really that surprising though. It brings to mind a meme. Imagine this; a cylinder is floating in a room. A light shining perpendicularly from one side of the room projects the shadow of a rectangle on the wall, while a light shining horizontally projects a circle on the opposite wall.

Two different perspectives; both are true.

Before we look at the equations here are a few notes ...

*There aren't any retrograde progression periods with this method, as there are in Secondary Progressions. For example, Mercury will be retrograde for most of us at some point in our Secondary Progressed chart. With Orbital Progressions, the retrograde movement is averaged in. We're not addressing retrogrades directly but instead looking at the big picture, the constant rate of revolution. We could say Secondary Progressions are the "true" calculation and Orbital Progressions are the "mean". It's fascinating to think that all this time, for centuries, there was a sister method to Secondary Progressions hiding in the shadows.

*Will you need an ephemeris to figure out Orbital Progressions? No, not that you shouldn't own one though! All you need is a little bit of math. This method is so ridiculously basic, yet incredibly beneficial. When you learn it you may have a good chuckle at its obviousness.

What exactly are Orbital Progressions?

*On the Ascendant - We are not progressing the Ascendant because we are using it as a marker of our entrance into this space/time. The moment we drew our first breath never changes, so for this method we are using it as an anchor point. We are not progressing the MC, IC, or Descendant either. Think of them as numbers on a clock face. They don't move. They remain stationary, allowing us to properly track time cycles.

*On the Moon - The Moon orbits the Sun at the same rate as the Earth. The Moon in this method moves a degree a year like it does with Solar Arcs.

*The outer planets and asteroids move too slowly to progress with this technique. Of course, their energy is always being factored in an evolutionary way, as their connection to and geometry with the progressed planets and asteroids changes.

*For basic, rounded calculation: if a person is a quarter through the year add .25, if halfway add .5, if three fourths add .75. For example, if someone is 45 years and 7 months at the time of a reading, then use 45.5 as their age. If someone is within a month of their next birthday, you may want to round up to their next age. (Integration with astrology software is coming, and it will offer exact, not rounded equations.)

*Whole Sign House system is being used; however, any house system can be used.

*Throughout the rest of this book, when O.P. appears, the Orbital Progression method is being referred to. When the "progressed" Sun is being referenced there is no distinction between Orbital Progressions/Secondary Progressions because they are the same.

*Other abbreviations being used:

NN - North Node

SN - South Node

PoF - Part of Fortune

Orbital Progression Equations

Planets

Mercury-

It takes mercury approximately 88 days to orbit the sun.

Mercury moves at a rate of 4.15 x's the rate of the Earth (Sun in chart).

It takes Mercury approximately 7.2 years to complete one sign by progression. Multiply person's age x's 4.15 to figure degrees to move progressed Mercury from natal Mercury.

Venus-

It takes Venus approximately 225 days to orbit the Sun.

Venus moves at a rate of 1.62 x's faster than the rate of Earth (Sun in chart).

It takes Venus approximately 18.5 years to complete one sign by progression. Multiply person's age x's 1.62 to figure degrees to move progressed Venus from natal Venus.

Earth (Sun in chart)-

It takes Earth approximately 365 days to orbit the Sun.

What exactly are Orbital Progressions?

It takes Earth approximately 30 years to complete a sign by progression.

Earth moves one degree per year (as seen with other progressed methods as well.)

Moon-

365 days to orbit the Sun.

Takes approximately 30 years to complete a sign by progression. The Moon moves one degree per year, as it travels with the Earth.

Mars-

It takes Mars approximately 687 days to orbit the Sun.

Mars moves at a rate of .53 slower than the rate of the Earth (Sun in chart). It takes Mars approximately 56.6 years to complete a sign by progression.

Multiply person's age x's .53 to figure degrees to move progressed Mars from natal Mars.

Jupiter-

It takes Jupiter approximately 4.330 days to orbit the Sun.

Jupiter moves at a rate of .08 slower than the rate of the Earth (Sun in chart). It takes Jupiter 375 years to complete a sign by progression.

Multiply person's age x's .08 to figure degrees to move progressed Jupiter from natal Jupiter.

Saturn-

It takes Saturn approximately 10,756 days to orbit the Sun.

Saturn moves at a rate of .03 slower than the rate of the Earth (Sun in chart). It takes Saturn 1,000 years to complete a sign by progression.

Multiply person's age x's .03 to figure degrees to move progressed Saturn from natal Saturn.

Asteroids

Vesta-

It takes Vesta approximately 1325 days to orbit the Sun.

Vesta moves at a rate of .28 slower than the Earth (Sun in chart). It takes Vesta 107 years to complete a sign by progression.

Multiply person's age x's .28 to figure degrees to move progressed Vesta from natal Vesta.

Juno-

It takes Juno approximately 1593 days to orbit the Sun.

Juno moves at a rate of .23 slower than the rate of the Earth (Sun in chart). It takes Juno 130.4 years to complete a sign by progression.

Multiply person's age x's .23 to figure degrees to move progressed Juno from natal Juno.

Ceres-

It takes Ceres approximately 1682 days to orbit the Sun.

Ceres moves at a rate of .22 slower than the Earth (Sun in chart). It takes Ceres 136.4 years to complete a sign by progression.

Multiply person's age x's .22 to figure degrees to move progressed Ceres from natal Ceres.

Pallas-

It takes Pallas approximately 1686 days to orbit the Sun. Pallas moves at a rate .22 slower than the Earth (Sun in chart). It takes Pallas 136.4 years to complete a sign by progression.

Multiply person's age x's .22 to figure degrees to move progressed Pallas from natal Pallas.

Part of Fortune

Moves one degree per year as it is calculated using Sun & Moon, each moving at that rate.

It takes approximately 30 years to complete a sign.

Example:

Let's say Mercury is at 19° Scorpio in the natal chart of a person born on Oct. 19, 1980. To find out where their OP Mercury was on Nov. 5, 2001. Take their age as of Nov. 5, in this case it would be 21 years old.

21 (age) x 4.15 (Mercury's rate of movement) = 87.15

Now advance Mercury 87° from its natal placement. In our example, that would place it at 16° Aquarius.

Case Studies

The following charts are a testament to the validity of Orbital Progressions. While it's impossible to understand what was fully going on in someone's chart and life without having a collaborative conversation with them, there is enough concrete information to demonstrate the accuracy of this technique.

Secondary progressed charts are included so we can do a side-by-side assessment of each. Occasionally, the degree points will sync up in both charts. For example, progressed Mars may be at the same degree in both charts. I've left descriptions of those aspects out so we can solely focus on the differences between the two techniques.

I hope you enjoy exploring these charts and seeing Orbital Progressions come to life.

Chapter 3
∙ ∙ ∙ ∙ ∙ ∙ ∙ ∙
Astrologers

Demetra George

If you've ever listened to Demetra George, one thing becomes evidently clear, she's brilliant. Her connection to the asteroids has opened a door for us all to better understand the sacred feminine qualities we each possess. Her ability to channel and disseminate the energy of these Divine cosmic bodies has brought balance to the energies that reside within the chart.

She offers up astrological ambrosia as she presents ancient mythical stories. Her tales sear their meaning into your mind. Her portrayal of these myths so powerfully invokes the archetypal energies that one can't help but to really feel them. As we fuse those feelings with specific cosmic bodies, our understanding of them exponentially deepens.

Her work spans beyond the asteroids, though. She has authored six books, her latest being Ancient Astrology in Theory and Practice. Being a highly respected maven in the field of astrology, it's no wonder she received the prestigious Regulus Award in Theory and Understanding.

The following chart is for the day she received the award: July 21, 2002.

She's spoken about her belief that astrology is akin to a burning flame of which gets passed from teacher to student as an initiatory right. Thousands of flames have been lit from her single candle; hence receiving this award. (O.P. Vesta exactly trine her Ascendant/O.P. Moon) (O.P. Vesta sextile her natal Moon/natal Uranus/NN/transit Saturn in Gemini/11th) (O.P. Mercury conjunct natal Vesta in the 9th/Aries)

It's not shocking that the award would be in acknowledgment of this astrologer's ability to channel messages of the goddesses. Demetra's brainchildren have expanded our understanding of how to utilize these energies. (Grand trine with O.P. Pallas, natal M.C. and natal/transit Venus) (O.P. Venus conjunct transit Pluto trine natal Uranus/Mercury/ASC/O.P. Moon)

The December 4, 2002 solar eclipse was at 12° Sagittarius conjunct O.P. Venus.

She's being recognized as a powerful leader and guru in astrological philosophy. (Grand trine with O.P. Mercury in Aries, O.P. Venus/transit Pluto and natal Sun/Pluto/transit Mars) (O.P. Mars exactly conjunct natal Jupiter in the 3rd, opposing O.P. Vesta in the 9th/Aries)

ORBITAL PROGRESSIONS
Age 56 (4 days before 56 Bday)

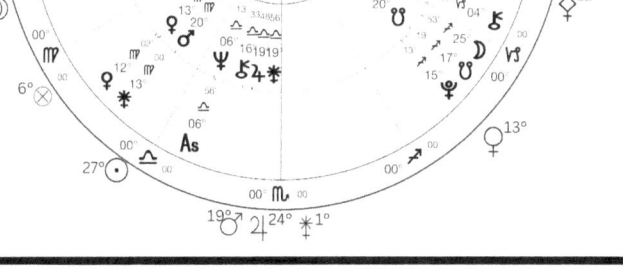

SECONDARY PROGRESSIONS

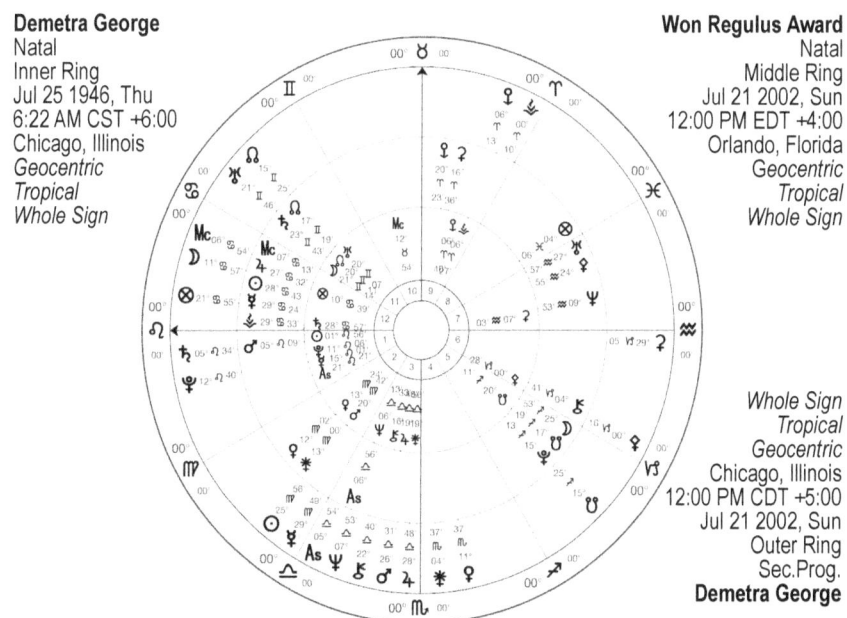

Chris Brennan

The work Chris wholeheartedly dedicates himself to has opened the door for many becoming astrologers. With his modest nature, you might not guess he's been such an astrology badass.

At a time when young astrologers were few and far between, he became President of the Association for Young Astrologers; he was 23. Down the road, he would start the Denver Astrology Group in an effort to support and educate those seeking a deep dive into the fathoms of astrology.

He's worked with Project Hindsight, served on the board of Kepler College, has been Research Director of the National Council of Geocosmic Research, was an associate editor of Mountain Astrologer Magazine, and authored Hellenistic Astrology: The study of Fate and Fortune. Okay, okay, Chris. We get it; you can stop with all the astrological accomplishments. You're making everyone else look bad.

The following chart is for the day he accepted the ISAR Award for Best Audio Podcast: Aug 30, 2022.

Have you listened to the Astrology Podcast? There's a lot of information there.

It's not shocking that he would take home an award for the over 365 episodes of astrological musings he's released over the past decade. (Grand trine between O.P. Mars, transit Mars/natal PoF in Gemini/5th, and O.P. Vesta/transit Mercury in the 9th) (Grand trine between O.P. Mercury in Aries/3rd, transit Venus in Leo, and natal Neptune)

The award pays tribute to Chris's ability to break down the mechanics, history, and philosophy of astrology into easily digestible pieces for astrology newbies, while synchronously engaging more experienced astrologers. (Progressed Moon conjunct transit Jupiter, trine natal MC, opposing O.P. Vesta/transit Mercury in the 9th).

His podcast demystifies astrology, allowing listeners to understand its practical application. (O.P. Mercury trine natal Neptune) Chris has thousands of listeners thinking of him as their astrology BFF. (Progressed Venus conjunct his Ascendant/transit Saturn, sextile natal Venus/Uranus in the 11th and progressed Sun). But would we really expect anything less from someone who has Venus conjunct Uranus in his Sag 11th?

ORBITAL PROGRESSIONS

Age 37.5

Chris Brennan
Natal
Inner Ring
Nov 1 1984, Thu
1:28 PM MST +7:00
Aurora,
Colorado
Geocentric
Tropical
Whole Sign

ISAR Award
Natal
Outer Ring
Aug 30 2022, Tue
7:00 PM MDT +6:00
Westminster,
Colorado
Geocentric
Tropical
Whole Sign

SECONDARY PROGRESSIONS

Chris Brennan
Natal
Inner Ring
Nov 1 1984, Thu
1:28 PM MST +7:00
Aurora,
Colorado
Geocentric
Tropical
Whole Sign

ISAR Award
Natal
Middle Ring
Aug 30 2022, Tue
7:00 PM MDT +6:00
Westminster,
Colorado
Geocentric
Tropical
Whole Sign

Whole Sign
Tropical
Geocentric
Aurora, Colorado
7:00 PM MDT +6:00
Aug 30 2022, Tue
Outer Ring
Sec.Prog.
Chris Brennan

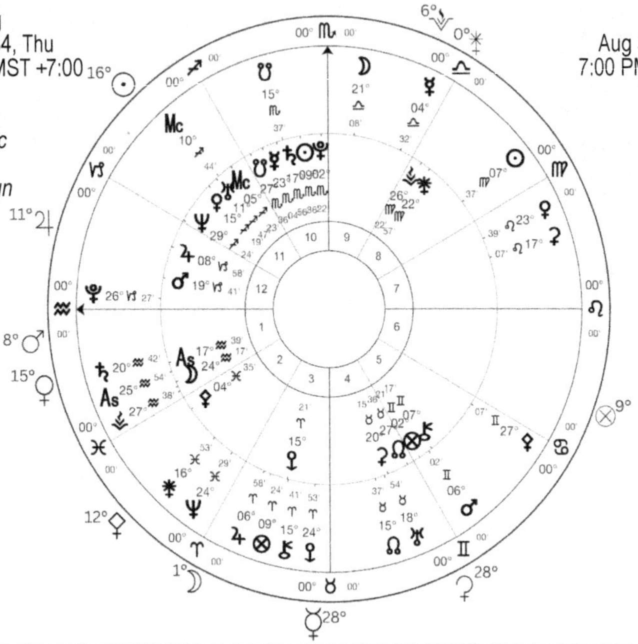

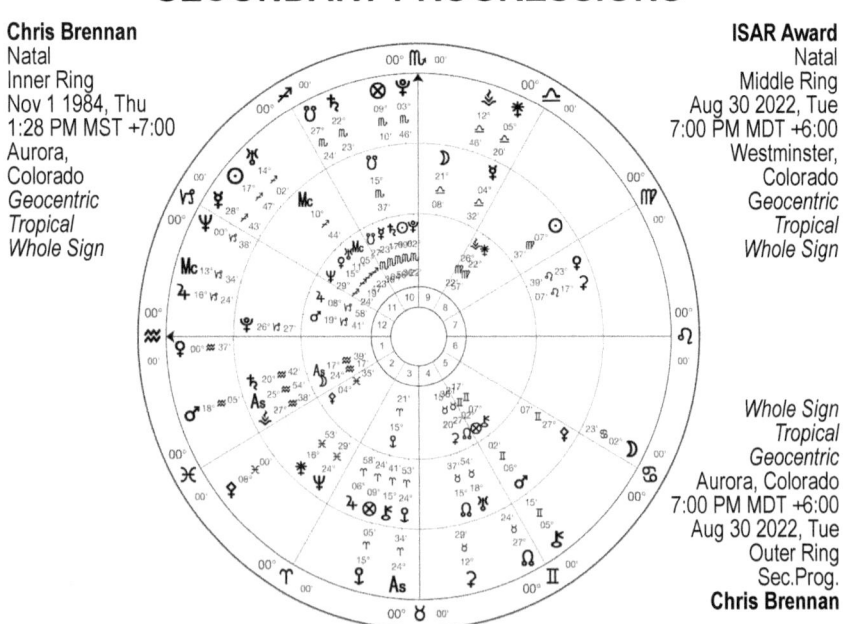

Liz Greene

Here we have a woman who has contributed greatly to the world of astrology; psychological astrology to be exact. In fact, she founded the Center for Psychological Astrology in London. By interweaving Jungian psychology with astrology, she helped to legitimize astrology as a form of psychotherapy.

But you may know her through her work with the founder of Astrodienst, a popular Swiss-based astrology site. When you pair an astrological genius with a brilliant, technological expert, you get Psychological Horoscope Analysis, the first computer generated chart interpretation of its kind. (I actually looked at a chart for this time period in her life and O.P. Mercury in Aquarius was conjunct transiting Jupiter and in opposition to natal Pluto.)

Artificial astrology intelligence, Astro Intelligence, was created to simulate Greene's own chart synthesis method. This was in the mid 1980's, talk about being on the leading edge. Still to this day you have your pick of her offerings including children's, vocational, and relationship horoscopes.

As if that weren't enough, she's also a prolific writer, having published a multitude of books. Saturn: A New Look at an Old Devil is one of her most influential. She did the ultimate P.R. work for Saturn with the release of the book. In my humble opinion, it's required reading for any astrologer who wants to not only understand the effects of this planetary energy in your life, but what must be done in order to balance the beast.

The following is the chart for the day her book Saturn was released: Jan 1, 1976.

It presented new and intellectually intriguing information. (O.P. Mercury, in the sign of Saturn, conjunct O.P. Pallas, trine to natal Mercury in the 11th house, sextile O.P. Mars/O.P. Jupiter/transit Uranus).

People appreciated its psychospiritual complexity. (O.P. Jupiter, ruler of the 5th, exactly conjunct natal Venus)

She became famous rather quickly with its publication. (O.P. Venus/transit Neptune/natal SN in a T-square with natal NN/natal Uranus/transit Sun in Gemini/ 8th, and natal Sun/MC) (O.P. Venus trine natal Pluto/transit Mars in the 10th)

ORBITAL PROGRESSIONS
Age 29.5

Liz Greene
Natal
Inner Ring
Sep 4 1946, Wed
1:01 PM EDT +4:00
Englewood,
New Jersey
Geocentric
Tropical
Whole Sign

Publication of Saturn
Natal
Outer Ring
Jun 1 1976, Tue
12:00 PM EDT +4:00
York Beach,
Maine
Geocentric
Tropical
Whole Sign

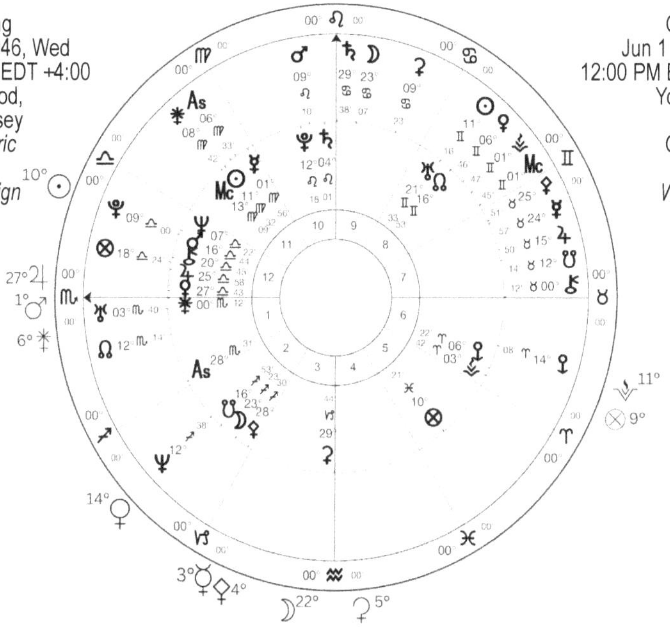

SECONDARY PROGRESSIONS

Liz Greene
Natal
Inner Ring
Sep 4 1946, Wed
1:01 PM EDT +4:00
Englewood,
New Jersey
Geocentric
Tropical
Whole Sign

Publication of Saturn
Natal
Middle Ring
Jun 1 1976, Tue
12:00 PM EDT +4:00
York Beach,
Maine
Geocentric
Tropical
Whole Sign

Whole Sign
Tropical
Geocentric
Englewood,
New Jersey
12:00 PM EDT +4:00
Jun 1 1976, Tue
Outer Ring
Sec.Prog.
Liz Greene

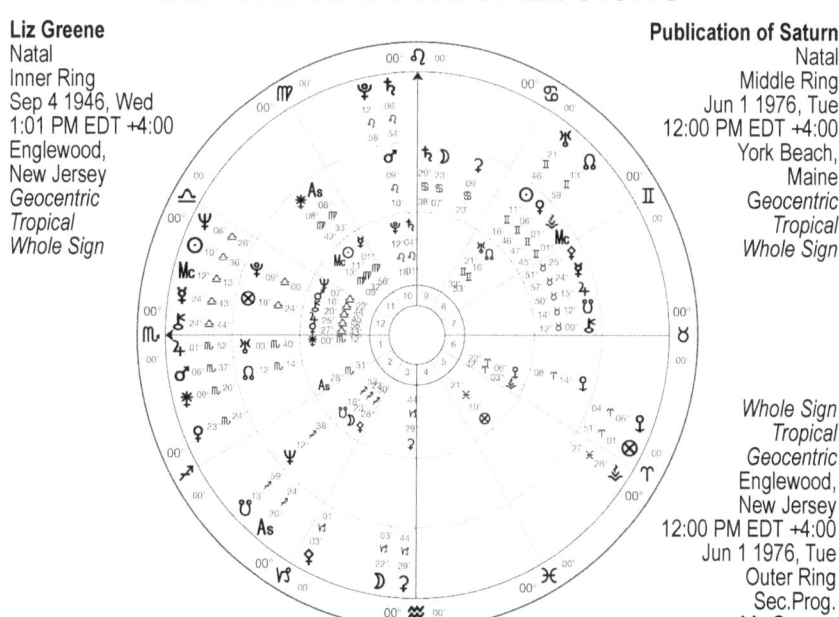

Lada Duncheva

This woman unwittingly helped me through my dark night of the soul. I've learned a lot from her throughout the years. Her Astrolada Youtube channel is a repository of astrological information with hundreds of videos to mine; hence it being one of the most popular astrology channels.

The scope of her knowledge is vast. She has an extensive background in diverse studies. She pulls from Hellenistic, Medieval, Babylonian, and Vedic traditions. She weaves complex interpretations but has the ability to present them in simplistic language so that even the greenest astrologers can understand.

The following chart is more general than other charts in this chapter, as it is for the year she began studying astrology as opposed to a specific day of an event.

Nonetheless, we can still use it to demonstrate Orbital alignments. We will just look at the slower moving planets.

In an interview with Kapiel Raj, she tells the story of how she was at the darkest part of her life when she was 23, which would have been in 2004. She was a hot mess, crying continuously, mentally depressed and with no direction. (O.P. Mercury conjunct transiting Saturn in Cancer squaring natal Mars/Mercury in Aries)

She's also having disastrous relationships with a man/men. (O.P. Mars opposing Juno in a cross with Ascendent/the Nodes) (O.P. Venus conjunct Pallas in the 5th opposing natal Uranus in Scorpio, squaring natal Vesta in the 7th) (O.P. Moon in the 8th opposing transit Vesta in Pisces)

So, she's in this bookstore when a book falls off the shelf in front of her. She picks it up, puts it back on the shelf and goes about her business. As she's leaving the store, the same book falls in front of her again. Being superstitious, she opens the book and the first sentence says, "If anyone is going through a dark night of the soul, they should study astrology and their horoscope to gain clarity and see when it will end."

With that, she began to seriously study astrology. (O.P. Mercury conjunct transit Saturn in the 6th; O.P. Venus conjunct Pallas trine natal Jupiter/Saturn in the 9th) It sent her in a new direction and on the path to developing a solid career in astrology. The Eclipse on Oct 8, 2004 was at 5° Taurus conjunct O.P. Mars, ruler of her 3rd/10th.

ORBITAL PROGRESSIONS
Age 23

Lada Duncheva
Natal
Inner Ring
Apr 14 1981, Tue
3:20 AM EEDT -3:00
Yambol,
Bulgaria
Geocentric
Tropical
Whole Sign

Begins Astrology Journey
Natal
Outer Ring
Jun 1 2004, Tue
12:00 PM BST -1:00
London,
United Kingdom
Geocentric
Tropical
Whole Sign

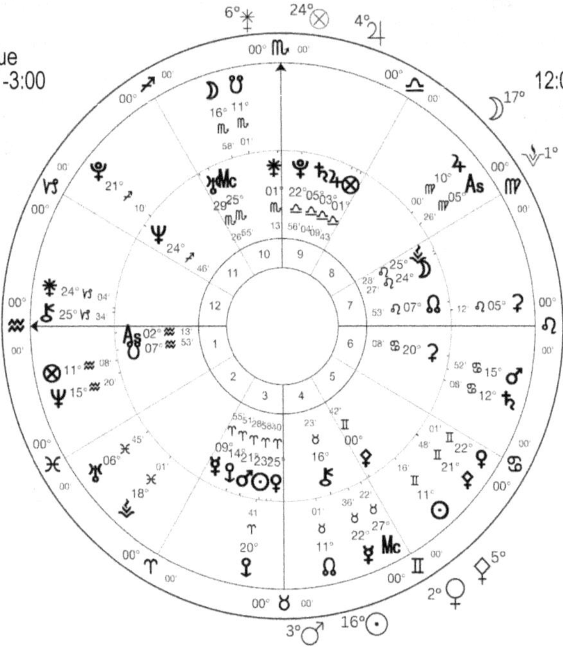

SECONDARY PROGRESSIONS

Lada Duncheva
Natal
Inner Ring
Apr 14 1981, Tue
3:20 AM EEDT -3:00
Yambol,
Bulgaria
Geocentric
Tropical
Whole Sign

Begins Astrology Journey
Natal
Middle Ring
Jun 1 2004, Tue
12:00 PM BST -1:00
London,
United Kingdom
Geocentric
Tropical
Whole Sign

Whole Sign
Tropical
Geocentric
Yambol,
Bulgaria
12:00 PM EEDT -3:00
Jun 1 2004, Tue
Outer Ring
Sec.Prog.
Lada Duncheva

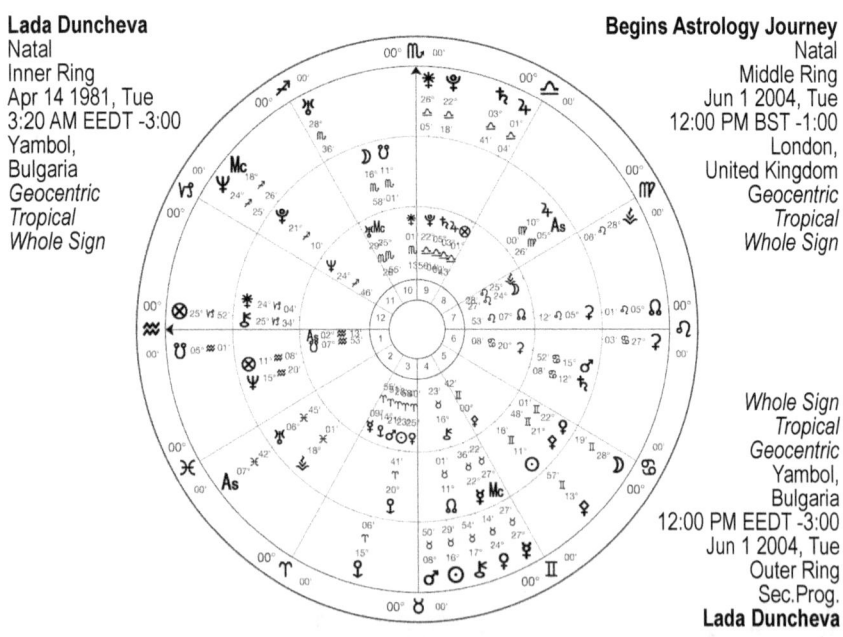

Robert E. Brown

It would only be fitting for me to include the astrologer with whom I had my gateway experience into the world of astrology.

It was 1996 and I found myself sitting across from Robert E. Brown, an adept astrologer who wrote a column for a popular New Age magazine, The Indigo Sun, in Houston. I had read plenty of horoscopes but had never had a reading so I was filled with curiosity. Was this dude really going to be able to accurately read my life with a chart? Ha, little did I know that he would become a revered astrology mentor to me down the road.

As I sat there with my newborn daughter, he started breaking down our current reality. My mind was pretty blown. He was on point, so I was all ears when he got to what was coming up next. He mentioned I should be careful driving. He saw a potential car accident.

Great, just what every new mom wants to hear. I wrote it off; "Clearly this man is crazy". Two weeks later, boom, a car accident. Now I would HAVE to know how he derived that, and everything else, from looking at my birth chart. It was the beginning of my astrological journey. I forever owe him a world of gratitude. (In that first meeting he also told me I was a writer. I laughed at the idea because I wasn't remotely interested, nor had I ever been, in writing anything. I was quite sure he was wrong… LOL)

The following chart is for the beginning of Robert's column, Writings In the Sky.

It was the threshold into full time astrology. (Grand trine between O.P. Mercury at 0° Aries, transit Pluto at 0° Sagittarius and natal

Uranus) He was writing for two pioneering women who started the publication. (O.P. Venus in Capricorn square natal Mercury/Pallas in the 10th, and sextile transit Saturn in the 3rd)

Writing for a popular magazine brought Robert many new clients (O.P. Mercury trine O.P. Jupiter) He could financially support himself and no longer needed a side hustle. (O.P. Mars exactly conjunct transit Uranus at 0° Aquarius/2nd, sextile transit Pluto, and opposing O.P. Jupiter) (O.P. Venus in Capricorn trine natal Moon/5th)

The eclipse on Oct 24, 1995 was at 0° Scorpio exactly conjunct his O.P. PoF, conjunct progressed Sun.

ORBITAL PROGRESSIONS

Age 40.5

Robert E. Brown
Natal
Inner Ring
Sep 16 1954, Thu
3:19 PM CST +6:00
Houston, Texas
Geocentric
Tropical
Whole Sign

Indigo Sun
Natal
Outer Ring
Apr 1 1995, Sat
12:00 PM CST +6:00
Houston, Texas
Geocentric
Tropical
Whole Sign

SECONDARY PROGRESSIONS

Robert E. Brown
Natal
Inner Ring
Sep 16 1954, Thu
3:19 PM CST +6:00
Houston, Texas
Geocentric
Tropical
Whole Sign

Indigo Sun
Natal
Middle Ring
Apr 1 1995, Sat
12:00 PM CST +6:00
Houston, Texas
Geocentric
Tropical
Whole Sign

Whole Sign
Tropical
Geocentric
Houston, Texas
12:00 PM CST +6:00
Apr 1 1995, Sat
Outer Ring
Sec.Prog.
Robert E. Brown

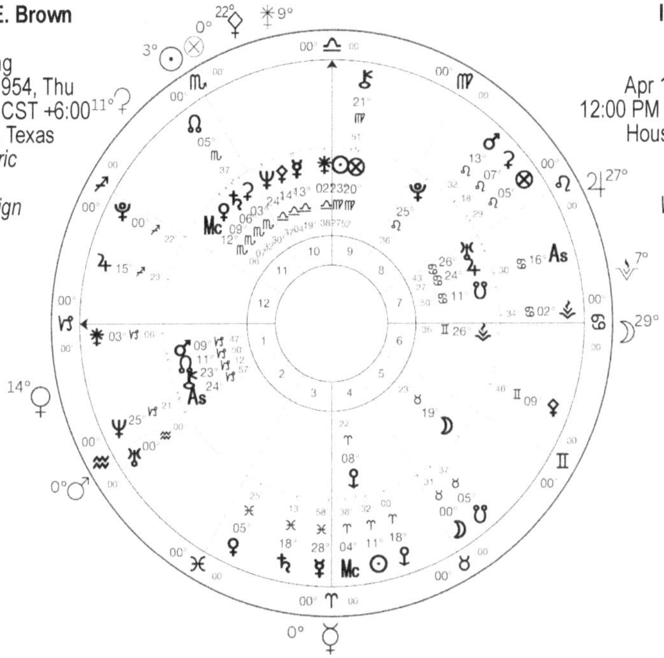

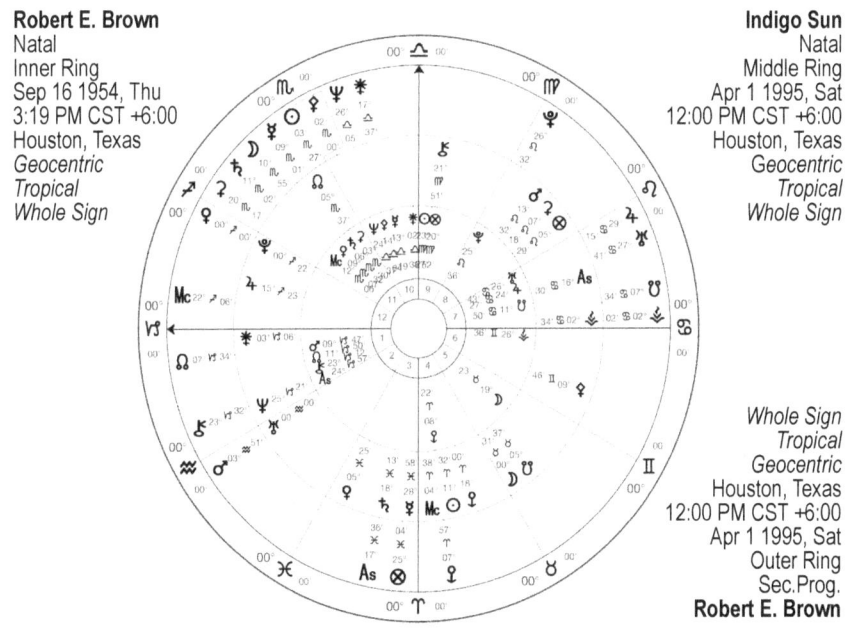

David Cochrane

Here we have the mad scientist of astrology. Doc, from Back to the Future comes to mind; sheer brilliance way ahead of the curve. The work David Cochrane has done with Vibrational Astrology is phenomenal and it's the future of astrology.

We are gaining a more dimensional perspective. Our lenses of perception are getting crisper, clearer, and more precise; look at the Hubble telescope vs. the James Webb. Astrology as a growing field of science is no different. It will be fine-tuned as we go and Vibrational Astrology is at the forefront.

We used to believe "junk" DNA served no purpose, or "empty" space was void of information. We now know those theories are incorrect. Both of those are actually brimming with information. Vibrational astrology is showing how aspects that have been considered unimportant, like mid-points or semisextiles, are actually key to understanding the underlying energies of a chart . David has also developed some of the most comprehensive astrology software in the world, Sirius and Kepler.

The following chart is for the day he won the Regulus Award for Discovery, Innovation, and Research: May 27, 2018.

He's being recognized for the discoveries he's made during his lengthy career in research astrology (Grand trine with O.P. Saturn/O.P. Venus/O.P. Ceres in the 6th, natal MC/transit Saturn/Vesta in the 10th, and natal Mars/transit Uranus/O.P. PoF)

He's being honored by his peers for Innovation. (O.P. Mars in Gemini/3rd exactly trine O.P. Jupiter Aquarius/11th) (O.P. Pallas opposing transit Pluto in the 10th, sextiling natal Mercury/transit Mercury) David puts astrology under a microscope, making the unseen seen. (O.P. Mercury conjunct transit Neptune trine Transit Jupiter in Scorpio/8th)

He has devoted his career to the study and development of Vibrational astrology in order to help astrologers understand the sacred geometric patterns which underlie a chart, much of which he has freely opened sourced online. He had been busy creating hundreds of videos for You Tube.(O.P. Vesta sextile O.P. Mercury/transit Neptune in the 12th; O.P. Vesta trine natal Sun/Venus in the 2nd) (O.P. Mars in Gemini/3rd trine Jupiter)

The July 27, 2018 lunar eclipse was at 4° Aquarius conjunct O.P. Jupiter.

ORBITAL PROGRESSIONS

Age 69

David Cochrane
Natal
Inner Ring
May 1 1949, Sun
4:26 AM EDT +4:00
East Meadow,
New York
Geocentric
Tropical
Whole Sign

Regulus Award
Event
Outer Ring
May 27 2018, Sun
7:00 PM CDT +5:00
Chicago,
Illinois
Geocentric
Tropical
Whole Sign

SECONDARY PROGRESSIONS

David Cochrane
Natal
Inner Ring
May 1 1949, Sun
4:26 AM EDT +4:00
East Meadow,
New York
Geocentric
Tropical
Whole Sign

Regulus Award
Event
Middle Ring
May 27 2018, Sun
7:00 PM CDT +5:00
Chicago,
Illinois
Geocentric
Tropical
Whole Sign

Whole Sign
Tropical
Geocentric
East Meadow,
New York
7:00 PM EDT +4:00
May 27 2018, Sun
Outer Ring
Sec.Prog.
David Cochrane

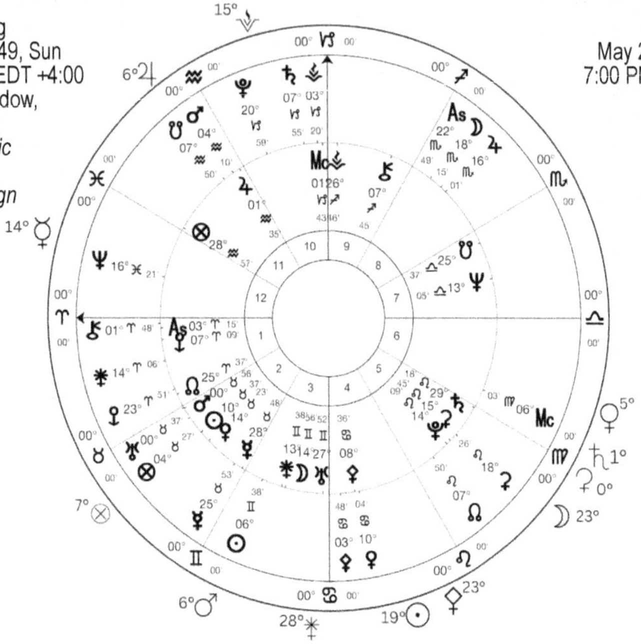

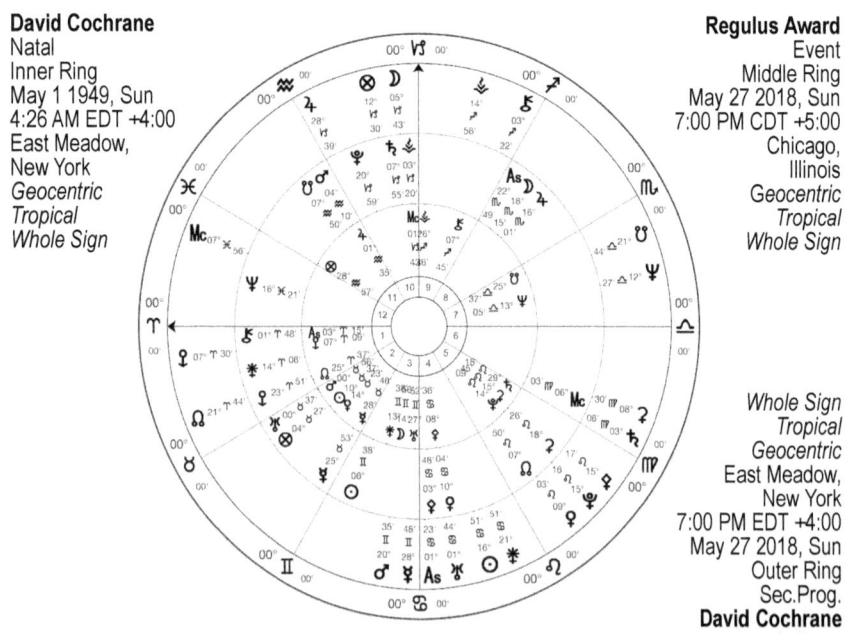

Adam Elenbaas

Adam Elenbaas has a heart-centered, philosophical approach to astrology. In his popular podcast, Nightlight Astrology, he mindfully yokes aspects to their deeper meanings for his listeners. There's a high level of sincerity, presence and thoughtfulness that comes through his recordings.

One episode in particular was especially touching as he announced that he would no longer be going by Acyuta-Bhava Das, a decision he didn't take lightly. He authentically opened up to share about his journey and assure his listeners that although his name was changing, his core values remain the same.

The following chart is for September 28, 2022, the day he formally announced that he was releasing his connection to the Hare Krishna tradition and the name Acyuta-Bhava.

He starts the podcast by saying he's been in deliberation for about a year and a half. His progressed Sun would have been exactly conjunct O.P. Ceres as he pondered returning to the identity his mother gave him. And his wife has held space and been supportive while he's been going through this process. (O.P. Venus conjunct natal Pluto/Juno trine O.P. Moon/transit Vesta)

He talks about devastating events that left a hole in his religious identity; and that his dad, the minister in his community, had a very public fall from his faith which was traumatic for him as a kid. (O.P. Mars conjunct natal Sun squaring transit Chiron)

Adam voices that the Hare Krishna tradition just doesn't feel like the right fit anymore. (O.P. Mercury conjunct natal Neptune in

Sagittarius, square transit Neptune, and inconjunct natal Sun) And, that his heart is no longer aligned with that path. (O.P. Venus, 1st house ruler, square Pluto in the 9th) (O.P. Mercury square natal vesta, transit Mercury (in retrograde) and Venus.)

The poignancy with which he speaks is indicative of the inner struggle and turmoil he's been feeling. (O.P. Moon/transit Saturn in a grand square with natal Uranus, natal Chiron/Asc/transit Uranus, and natal Venus/Ceres) The lunar Eclipse on May 15th was at 25°Scorpio, squaring the O.P. Moon and activating that fixed grand cross.

He pays homage to the teachers and texts that have been a valued part of his spiritual journey. He's transmuting a spiritual layer he has outgrown, like a phoenix from the ashes of a consecrated fire. (O.P. Vesta conjunct natal Jupiter/Saturn Opposing transit Jupiter, squaring natal Mercury)

ORBITAL PROGRESSIONS
Age 41

Adam Elenbaas
Natal
Inner Ring
Jul 16 1981, Thu
2:32 AM EDT +4:00
Lexington,
Kentucky
Geocentric
Tropical
Whole Sign

Return to Birth Name
Event
Outer Ring
Sep 28 2022, Wed
12:00 PM CDT +5:00
Minneapolis,
Minnesota
Geocentric
Tropical
Whole Sign

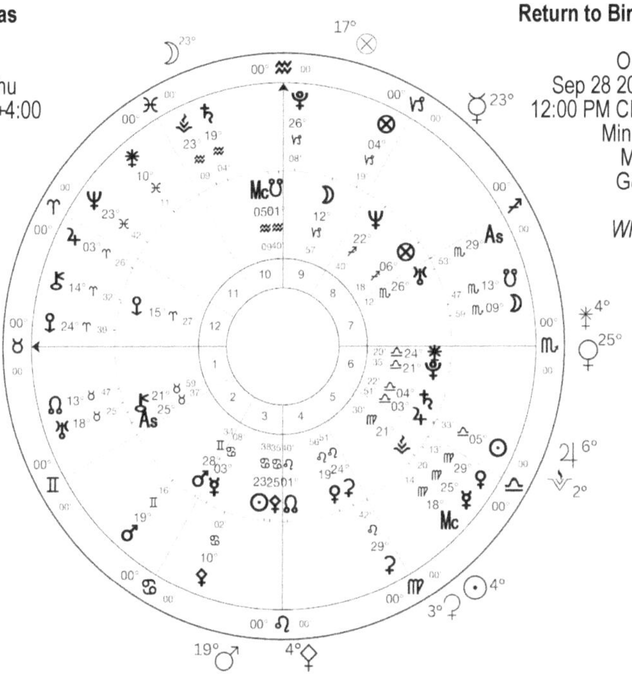

SECONDARY PROGRESSIONS

Adam Elenbaas
Natal
Inner Ring
Jul 16 1981, Thu
2:32 AM EDT +4:00
Lexington,
Kentucky
Geocentric
Tropical
Whole Sign

Return to Birth Name
Event
Middle Ring
Sep 28 2022, Wed
12:00 PM CDT +5:00
Minneapolis,
Minnesota
Geocentric
Tropical
Whole Sign

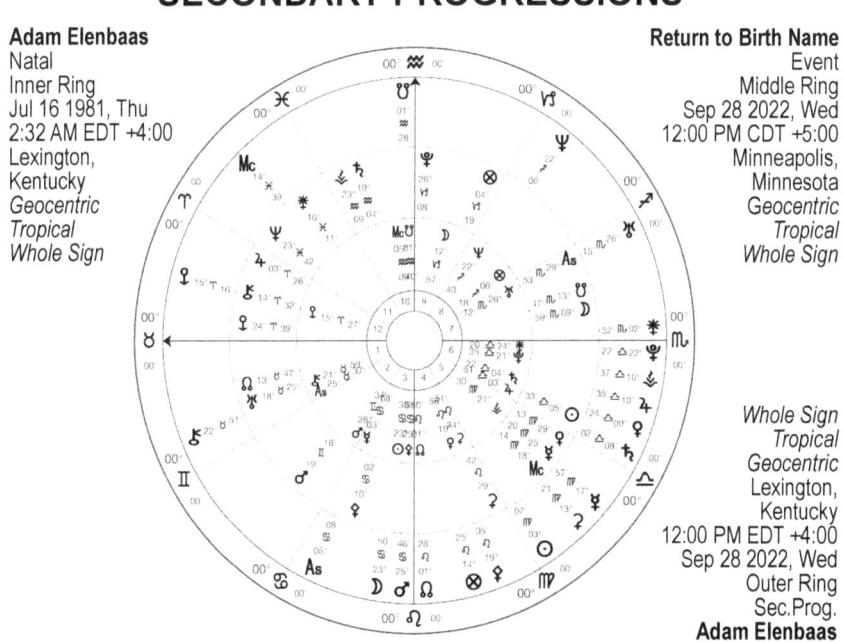

Whole Sign
Tropical
Geocentric
Lexington,
Kentucky
12:00 PM EDT +4:00
Sep 28 2022, Wed
Outer Ring
Sec.Prog.
Adam Elenbaas

Chapter 4

Athletes with Dramatic Identity Shifts

I can't pretend to be a sports fanatic. I avoided P.E. like the plague. But, the two athletes that follow created shock and awe in the masses for reasons both on and off the field...

Caitlyn Jenner (Formerly known as Bruce Jenner)

Which is flashing through your mind, the Wheaties box or a reality T.V. series? If it's the latter, congratulations on your youth. Long before the media circus of the Kardashians, this human-being dazzled and inspired the masses with spectacular athletic abilities. In 1976 he broke the world record and won gold for the Olympic decathlon in thrilling and dramatic form.

Nowadays, he inspires others with his courage in a whole different arena. At a time when so many are struggling to figure out who they are, Caitlyn Jenner has stepped forward in transparency to be an example of self-integrity; not to push a transgender agenda but to simply show it's ok to be yourself, whoever that self may be.

Transgender or not, aren't we all on a mission to live life authentically? Reinventing ourselves is the story of our soul's journey throughout eternity.

"There's nothing more, nothing better, in life than to wake up in the morning, look at yourself in the mirror, and feel comfortable with yourself and who you are." Caitlyn Jenner. We all strive for this in one way or another.

The following is the chart for the day Caitlyn Jenner made a big announcement, revealing a shocking secret about her feminine nature and change in sexual orientation. (Cardinal Grand Cross between O.P. Mercury/transit Venus in Cancer, natal Mercury/O.P. Pallas/SN in the Libra/12th, transit Pluto/natal Jupiter, and transit Uranus/NN) Sadly, death threats were received. We can see that in those aspects as well.

She is having a complete and total identity shift from masculine to feminine. (Grand Cross between O.P. Venus/O.P. Moon, O.P. Mars/natal Pallas, progressed Sun/natal Vesta, and natal Uranus)

She's working to nurture and heal a core wound around self-worth. (O.P. Venus/O.P. Moon trine natal Chiron/transit Saturn)

The September 27, 2015 lunar eclipse was at 4° Aries conjunct O.P. Venus/O.P. Moon.

ORBITAL PROGRESSIONS

Age 65.5

Caitlyn Jenner
Natal
Inner Ring
Oct 28 1949, Fri
6:16 AM EST +5:00
Mount Kisco,
New York
Geocentric
Tropical
Whole Sign

Announced Caitlyn
Natal
Outer Ring
Jun 1 2015, Mon
12:00 PM PDT +7:00
Malibu, California
Geocentric
Tropical
Whole Sign

SECONDARY PROGRESSIONS

Caitlyn Jenner
Natal
Inner Ring
Oct 28 1949, Fri
6:16 AM EST +5:00
Mount Kisco,
New York
Geocentric
Tropical
Whole Sign

Announced Caitlyn
Natal
Middle Ring
Jun 1 2015, Mon
12:00 PM PDT +7:00
Malibu, California
Geocentric
Tropical
Whole Sign

Whole Sign
Tropical
Geocentric
Mount Kisco,
New York
12:00 PM EDT +4:00
Jun 1 2015, Mon
Outer Ring
Sec.Prog.
Caitlyn Jenner

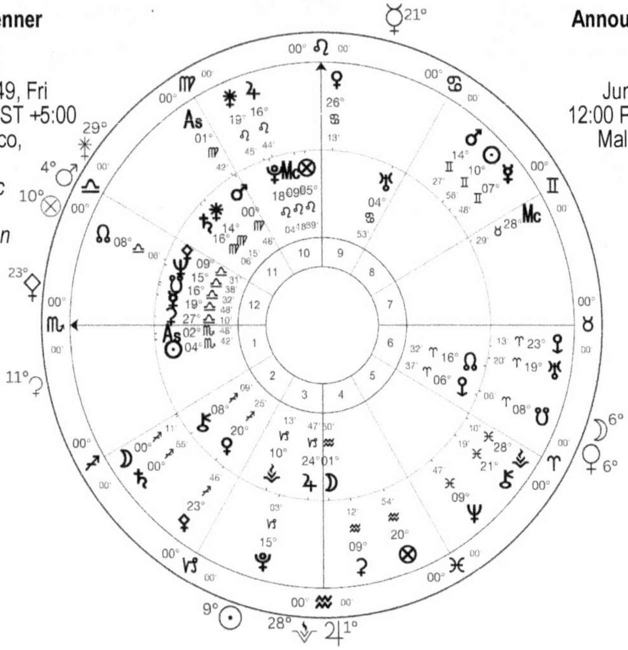

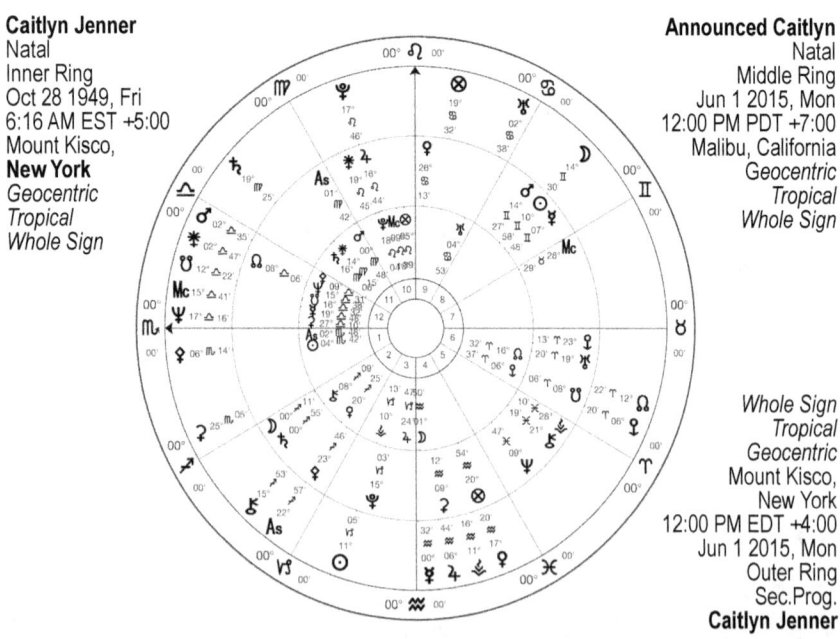

O.J. Simpson

The mere mention of this person's name is enough to make people wince. I approach this subject with caution, as opinions vary greatly, and respect for the families involved. Ultimately, whatever happened is between him and his higher power. It's a tragic tale, no matter how you spin it; one that had the world astonished as they watched the dramatic and the unthinkable unfold.

On June 17th 1994 a police chase with a white Ford Bronco down a southern California highway was breaking news. The most shocking element was the identity of the passenger, O.J. Simpson, the "Juice". All were watching as the Hall of Famer, sports broadcaster, and beloved football icon, fled as a fugitive.

The following chart is of the moment of the chase: June 17, 1994.

The charge was for the murder of his ex-wife, Nicole Brown Simpson, and her boyfriend, Ron Goldman, in a crime of passion. (T-square with O.P. Mars exactly conjunct natal Venus/ O.P. Vesta in the 12th opposing O.P. Juno and squaring natal Moon conjunct O.P. Pallas, 8th house, Pisces)

The mother of his children was taken from them. (O.P. Ceres conjunct O.P. Moon in T-square with natal Saturn/Pluto and transit Jupiter in Scorpio) If you're not familiar with the mythology of Ceres, in a nutshell, it's a story of a daughter, Persephone, being taken from her mother, Ceres, by Pluto in swift and violent action.

This was headline news which severely tarnished his reputation and created infamy. (O.P. Mercury opposing natal Sautrn/Uranus in the 1st/Leo)

He was acquitted for the murders in 1995. Interestingly, the April 29, 1995 solar eclipse was at 9° Taurus conjunct O.P. Ceres.

However, he was found guilty in the civil lawsuit and was ordered to pay 33 million to the families of his ex-wife and her partner. (Mutable Grand Cross between O.P. Part of Fortune, natal Juno, O.P. Venus, and natal Moon)

The civil suit ended in 1997. The solar eclipse on March 9, 1997 at 18° Pisces in opposition to O.P. Venus. The lunar eclipse on Sept. 16, 1997 at 23° Pisces was conjunct O.P. Pallas in the 8th, square O.P. PoF.

ORBITAL PROGRESSIONS
Age 47 (3 weeks til 47th birthday)

OJ Simpson
Natal
Inner Ring
Jul 9 1947, Wed
8:08 AM PST +8:00
San Francisco
Geocentric
Tropical
Whole Sign

Bronco Chase
Natal
Outer Ring
Jun 17 1994, Fri
6:00 PM PDT +7:00
Los Angeles, California
Geocentric
Tropical
Whole Sign

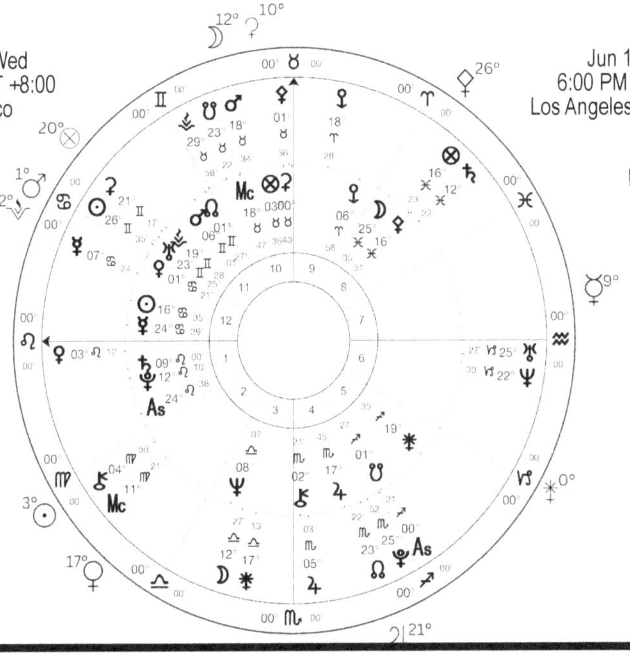

SECONDARY PROGRESSIONS

OJ Simpson
Natal
Inner Ring
Jul 9 1947, Wed
8:08 AM PST +8:00
San Francisco
Geocentric
Tropical
Whole Sign

Bronco Chase
Natal
Middle Ring
Jun 17 1994, Fri
6:00 PM PDT +7:00
Los Angeles, California
Geocentric
Tropical
Whole Sign

Whole Sign
Tropical
Geocentric
San Francisco
6:00 PM PDT +7:00
Jun 17 1994, Fri
Outer Ring
Sec.Prog.
OJ Simpson

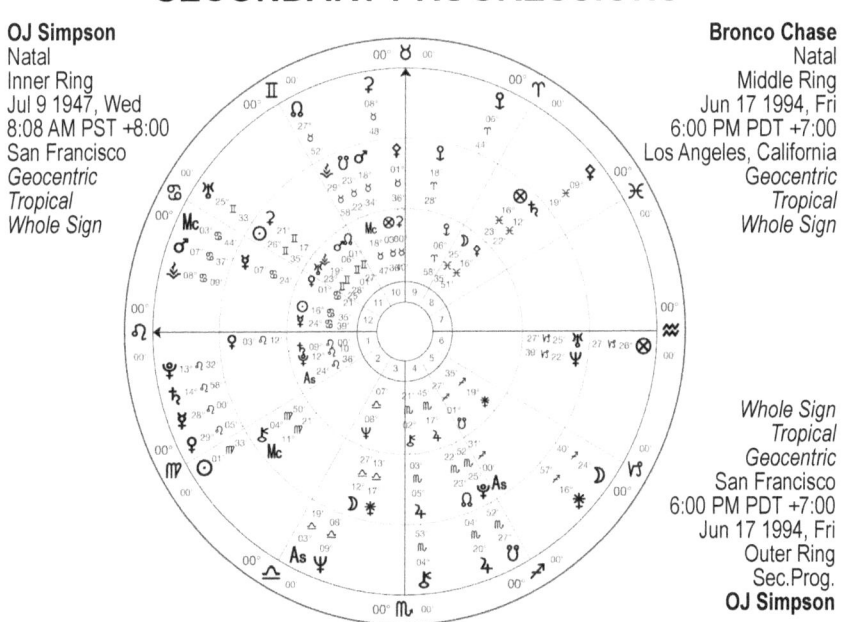

Chapter 5
• • • • • • • •
Authors

Stephen King

Many of us know Stephen King as a nightmare novelist, one who brings forth the plight of the weird and wicked. Having the natal ruler of the 8th/Uranus, in the 12th/Gemini, naturally endows him with the ability to produce chronicles of some seriously twisted, supernatural shit.

I had seen plenty of movies based on his writings but had never actually read one of his books; that is, until I took a Kepler class: Writing for Publication. My teachers, Arlan Wise and Alexandra Karacostas, encouraged us to read a Stephen King book, On Writing. It was not about the horrific, unless you count the true rendition of his gruesome encounter with a van that almost left him for dead. Rather, it was a biographical account of his life with the wisdom he's gleaned on his journey to being a famous author. It's honest, no bullshit advice on how to write blunt but engaging content, appropriate for an Aries 10th house wouldn't you say?

One of the stories he includes is of how Carrie came to be. The following chart is of Carrie's release: April 5, 1974.

Authors

Stephen wrote the beginning of Carrie then tossed it in the trash because he couldn't identify with the main character, a tortured teenage girl, only to come home to all the crumpled pages laid back out by wife, who insisted he keep going. (O.P. Juno in exact opposition to his Uranus in Gemini) Side note: turns out Stephen King is quite a romantic, completely in love with his wifey muse. It's surprisingly endearing for this harbinger of horror.

He was young and broke, living with his wife and two kids in a podunk town. She worked at the donut shop. He taught high school and worked at a laundromat, writing during any extra time he managed to find. They would have been psyched for $40,000, and needless to say, they were aghast when Carrie delivered a $400,000 royalty check to their doorstep. (O.P. Venus in a T-square with Natal Pluto and Part of Fortune + a grand trine between O.P. Mercury, O.P. Part of Fortune, and natal Venus)

Carrie is a tale of a girl with telekinetic power who seeks brutal and bloody revenge on all those who ceaselessly tormented her. (O.P. Mercury/transit Pallas in the 8th/Aquarius, in opposition to O.P. Mars) (O.P. Mars in Scorpio square natal Pluto/Saturn/O.P. Mars) The Nov 29, 1974 lunar eclipse was at 7° Gemini exactly conjunct O.P. PoF.

ORBITAL PROGRESSIONS
Age 26

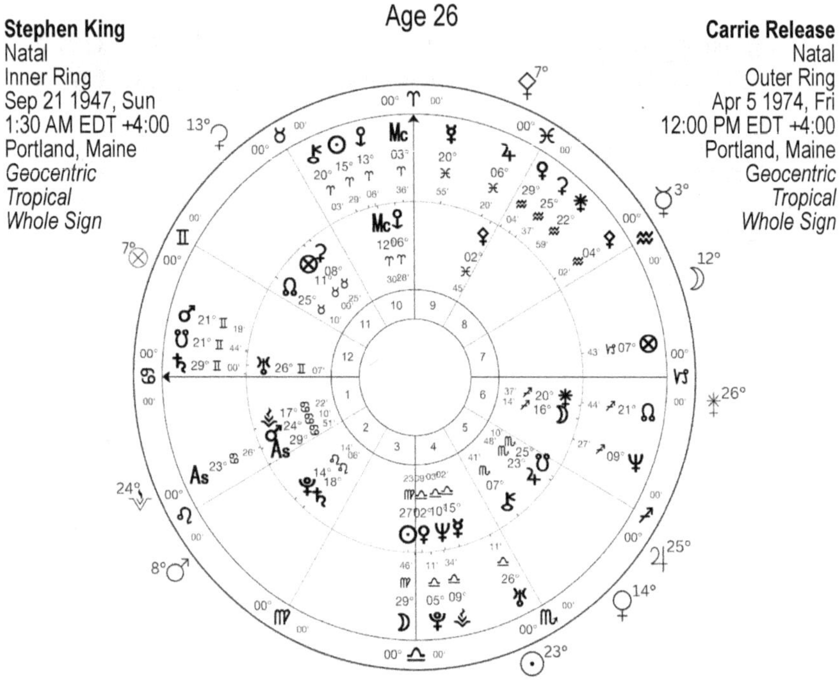

Stephen King
Natal
Inner Ring
Sep 21 1947, Sun
1:30 AM EDT +4:00
Portland, Maine
Geocentric
Tropical
Whole Sign

Carrie Release
Natal
Outer Ring
Apr 5 1974, Fri
12:00 PM EDT +4:00
Portland, Maine
Geocentric
Tropical
Whole Sign

SECONDARY PROGRESSIONS

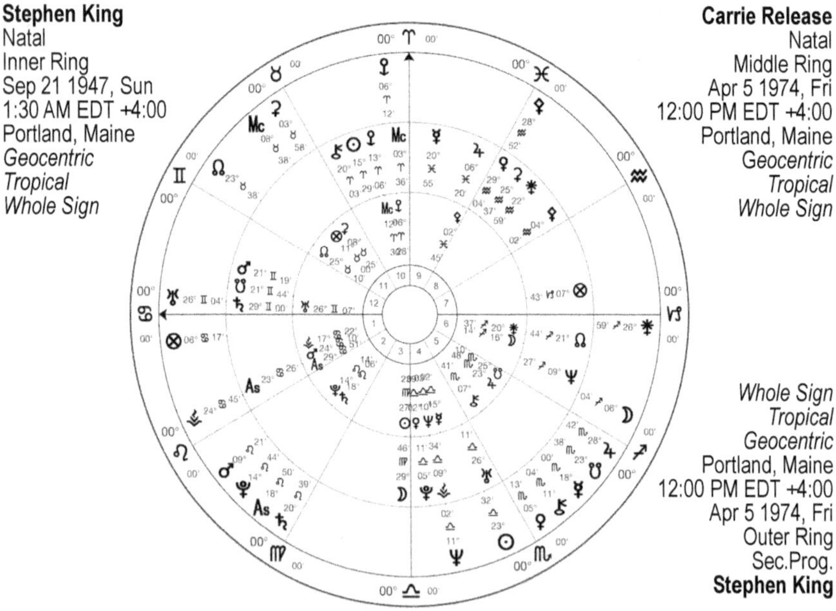

Stephen King
Natal
Inner Ring
Sep 21 1947, Sun
1:30 AM EDT +4:00
Portland, Maine
Geocentric
Tropical
Whole Sign

Carrie Release
Natal
Middle Ring
Apr 5 1974, Fri
12:00 PM EDT +4:00
Portland, Maine
Geocentric
Tropical
Whole Sign

Whole Sign
Tropical
Geocentric
Portland, Maine
12:00 PM EDT +4:00
Apr 5 1974, Fri
Outer Ring
Sec.Prog.
Stephen King

J.K. Rowling

The inspirational rags-to-riches story of J.K. Rowling, creatrix extraordinaire, is one of total dedication and tireless perseverance. Her Potter prose pulls us into the fantastical world of a boy sorcerer, who discovers his inner power alongside his best mates at a magical school for wizards. (O.P. Mercury trine natal Pluto/Uranus in the 8th)

The following chart is for the day her first book, Harry Potter and the Sorcerer's Stone, was released: June 26, 1997.

The book was an "overnight success" (O.P. Mercury trine natal Uranus) but Rowling has been refreshingly real about her life at the time Harry Potter and the Sorcerer's Stone was released.

She was dealing with bouts of depression which left her feeling isolated. In a later book, she would use that experience to create "Dementors". (O.P. Mercury in the 12th, Capricorn square transit Saturn)

She was a single mother who mostly wrote in a coffee shop while her daughter napped in the pram next to her. (O.P. Mercury square O.P. Ceres in the 3rd/Aries)

At the time she was broke and living in subsidized housing (O.P. Venus/O.P. Moon square Neptune in the 12th/Capricorn)

Little did she know her whole financial world was about to reset. She was launching into a whole new financial chapter of which would bring her an absurd amount of money, more than her wildest dreams. At this point she's reached billionaire status. (O.P.

Part of Fortune at 0°/1st conjunct transit Neptune/Pallas/Uranus, opposing transit Venus, and sextiling Pluto/11th)

She received 12 rejection notices from publishers before Harry Potter got picked up. (O.P. Mercury T-square with transit Saturn in the 3rd and natal Mars in the 9th)

Her commitment paid off though, she accrued a multitude of awards and this book alone has sold over 120 million copies. Eventually she would become one of the best-selling authors of all time. (O.P. Vesta conjunct O.P. Jupiter in Gemini/5th, trine O.P. Venus/O.P. Moon in the 9th) The lunar eclipse of September 16, 1997 was at 24° Pisces, exactly square O.P. Jupiter)

ORBITAL PROGRESSIONS
Age 32 (one month til B-Day)

J.K. Rowling
Natal
Inner Ring
Jul 31 1965, Sat
9:10 PM BST -1:00
Yate,
United Kingdom
Geocentric
Tropical
Whole Sign

Harry Potter Release
Natal
Outer Ring
Jun 26 1997, Thu
12:00 PM BST -1:00
London,
United Kingdom
Geocentric
Tropical
Whole Sign

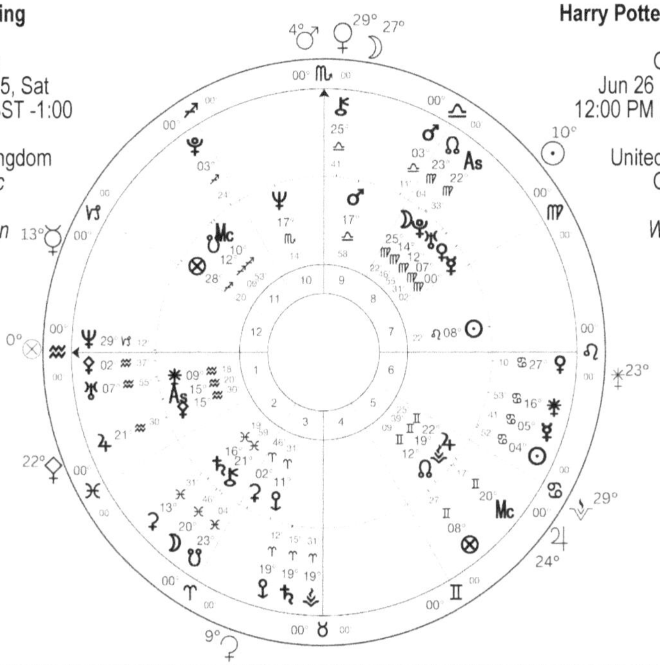

SECONDARY PROGRESSIONS

J.K. Rowling
Natal
Inner Ring
Jul 31 1965, Sat
9:10 PM BST -1:00
Yate,
United Kingdom
Geocentric
Tropical
Whole Sign

Harry Potter Release
Natal
Middle Ring
Jun 26 1997, Thu
12:00 PM BST -1:00
London,
United Kingdom
Geocentric
Tropical
Whole Sign

Whole Sign
Tropical
Geocentric
Yate,
United Kingdom
12:00 PM BST -1:00
Jun 26 1997, Thu
Outer Ring
Sec.Prog.
J.K. Rowling

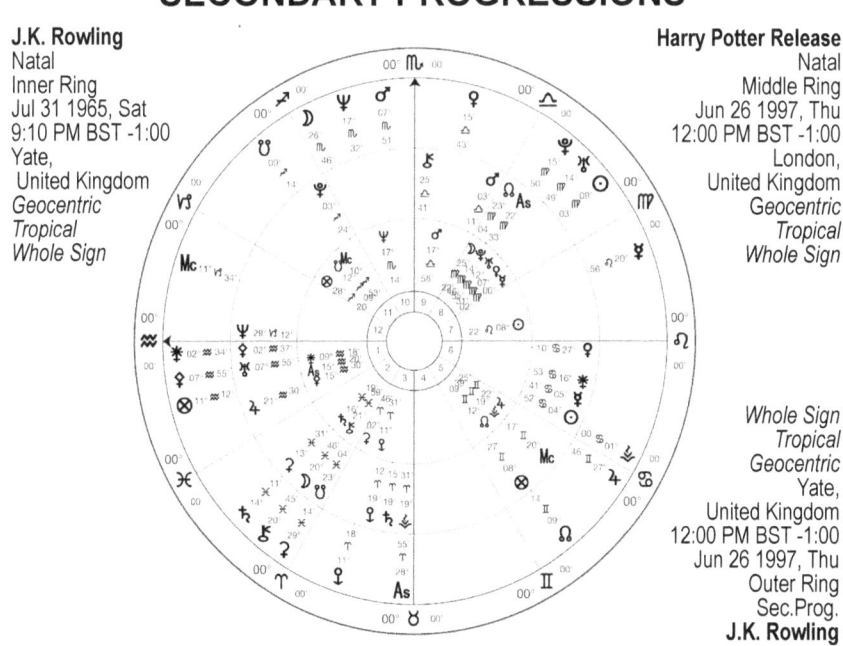

Chapter 6
∙ ∙ ∙ ∙ ∙ ∙ ∙ ∙
Births

Ricki Lake: The Business of being Born

Ricki Lake is a television host/actress who is known for Hairspray, Cry-Baby, and Serial Mom, and her daytime talk show, but perhaps her most profound work is the movie, The Business of Being Born. It shines a light on modern practices in obstetrics that may be detrimental to the health and wellbeing of mothers and babies.

The following chart is for the release of The Business of Being Born on Jan 9, 2008.

In an interview with Huffington Post, Ricki shared her intention for this film, "I hope this film educates people and empowers them to really know their choices in childbirth." She also co-authored a book on the topic. (O.P. Venus conjunct transit Pluto in the 3rd, opposing transit Mars; O.P. Moon conjunct natal Venus/Mercury/Pallas)

She was inspired to create a documentary based upon her personal experience with birth. She talks about how she had intended to have a natural birth with her first child, but feeling uniformed and underprepared, she fell into the experience of modern American interventions. (O.P. Mercury conjunct natal Chiron square O.P. Venus/transit Pluto) Her second was a completely opposite experience, at home with a midwife.

The Business of Being Born questions standard birth practices in hospitals and brings to light changes that could be made in order to improve maternity care in the U.S. (O.P. Mars in the 12th, conjunct natal Pluto, trine transit Sun in the 4th)

It discusses the trauma that can be created through unnatural interventions. (O.P. Mars in the 12th opposing transit Uranus in the 6th)

Ricki sees herself as an advocate for women's reproductive and birthing rights. (O.P. Vesta conjunct transit Ceres in the 8th; O.P. Venus trine natal Mars in Leo)

*Bringing a baby into this world is a powerful experience no matter how it unfolds. The way a woman gives birth is just as unique as the woman herself. As astrologers, we are able to gain much insight when we look at the mother's progressed chart at the time of her child's birth. It will show things like how she is apt to deal with postpartum and how she will bond and interact with her child.

ORBITAL PROGRESSIONS

Age 39

Ricki Lake
Natal
Inner Ring
Sep 21 1968, Sat
8:00 AM EDT +4:00
Hastings,
New York
Geocentric
Tropical
Whole Sign

B of Being Born
Natal
Outer Ring
Jan 9 2008, Wed
12:00 PM EST +5:00
Manhattan,
New York
Geocentric
Tropical
Whole Sign

SECONDARY PROGRESSIONS

Ricki Lake
Natal
Inner Ring
Sep 21 1968, Sat
8:00 AM EDT +4:00
Hastings,
New York
Geocentric
Tropical
Whole Sign

B of Being Born
Natal
Middle Ring
Jan 9 2008, Wed
12:00 PM EST +5:00
Manhattan,
New York
Geocentric
Tropical
Whole Sign

Whole Sign
Tropical
Geocentric
Hastings,
New York
12:00 PM EST +5:00
Jan 9 2008, Wed
Outer Ring
Sec.Prog.
Ricki Lake

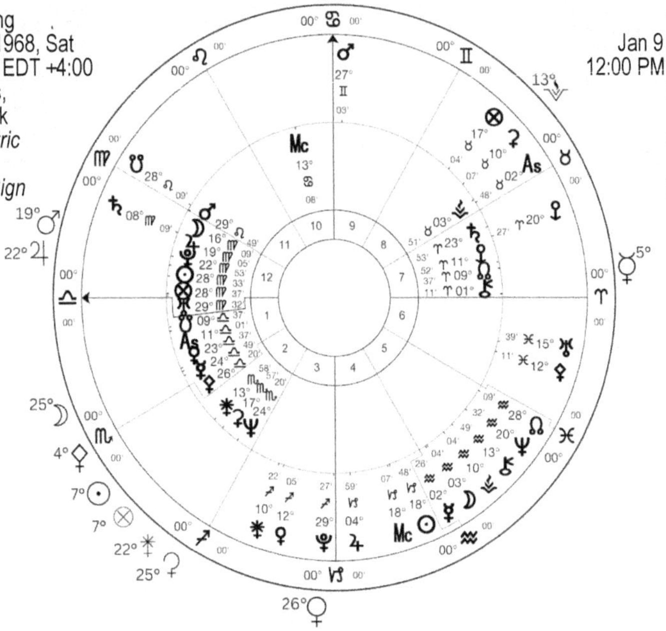

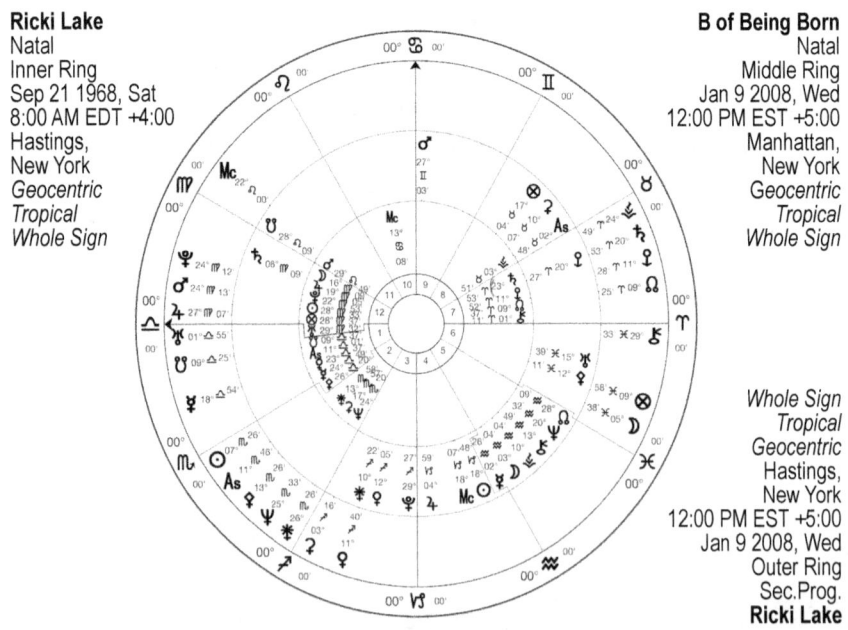

Births

Let's do something a little different here...

With the two following charts, we are looking at the dynamics at play between a mother's natal chart, the mother's O.P. progressed chart, and her child's natal chart. It is absolutely fascinating, but not surprising, to see how well these tell the story of what their relationships would become.

The following charts demonstrate a mother/daughter relationship of an easy nature and one of a difficult nature.

Goldie Hawn/Kate Hudson

Goldie and Kate are like two peas in a pod. They've had a harmonious relationship from the start and have remained tightly woven throughout life's journey. They just sincerely enjoy each other's company. Currently Goldie lives around the corner from Kate so that they can be involved in day-to-day activities of life.

The following chart is for Kate's birth, April 19, 1979.

In an interview with People, Kate said, "My mom gave me the floor to be able to feel confident enough to go out and feel like my life could be my own. Mom was my greatest cheerleader." (Goldie's O.P. Mercury in Grand trine with Kate's Saturn/Goldie's O.P. Venus/Sun)

Kate has also discussed how her mom has always been her confidante; how she tells her everything, and appreciates the insight Goldie shares. (Goldie's O.P. Mars in Leo trine O.P. Ceres/natal Mercury/Kate's Neptune) (Kate's Mercury trine Goldie's O.P. Pallas)

"My mom has always been an inspiration to me and, in so many ways, the foundation for my values. There's no doubt that I inherited her love for life and all of its experiences, big and small." Kate Hudson (Goldie's O.P. Pallas trine Kate's Venus/Mercury and Jupiter) (Goldie's O.P. PoF trine Kate's PoF)

"Mom always said to me, 'Don't you ever let a man dim your light,'" Kate Hudson. (Grand trine between Goldie's O.P. Pallas, Natal Mars and Kate's Vesta) (Kate's Sun trine Goldie's O.P. Vesta)

ORBITAL PROGRESSIONS

Age 33

Goldie Hawn
Natal
Inner Ring
Nov 21 1945, Wed
9:20 AM EST +5:00
Washington
Geocentric
Tropical
Whole Sign

Kate Hudson
Natal
Outer Ring
Apr 19 1979, Thu
10:51 AM PST +8:00
Los Angeles, California
Geocentric
Tropical
Whole Sign

SECONDARY PROGRESSIONS

Goldie Hawn
Natal
Inner Ring
Nov 21 1945, Wed
9:20 AM EST +5:00
Washington
Geocentric
Tropical
Whole Sign

Kate Hudson
Natal
Middle Ring
Apr 19 1979, Thu
10:51 AM PST +8:00
Los Angeles, California
Geocentric
Tropical
Whole Sign

Whole Sign
Tropical
Geocentric
Washington
10:51 AM +0:00
Apr 19 1979, Thu
Outer Ring
Sec.Prog.
Goldie Hawn

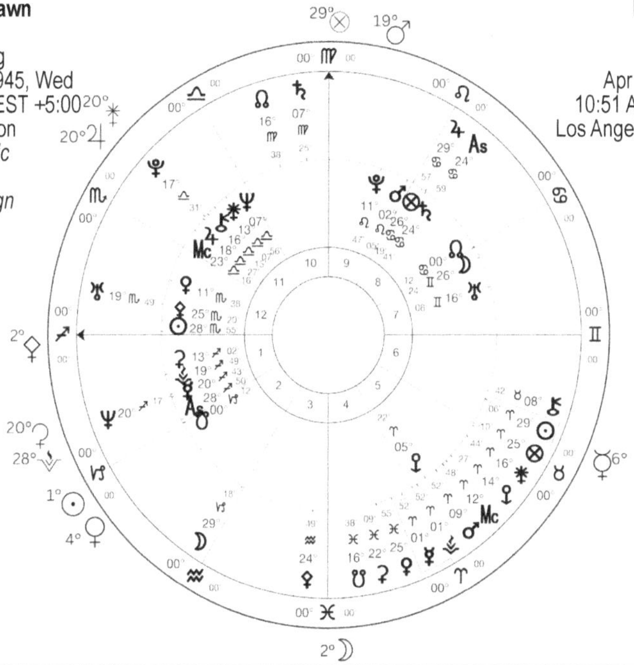

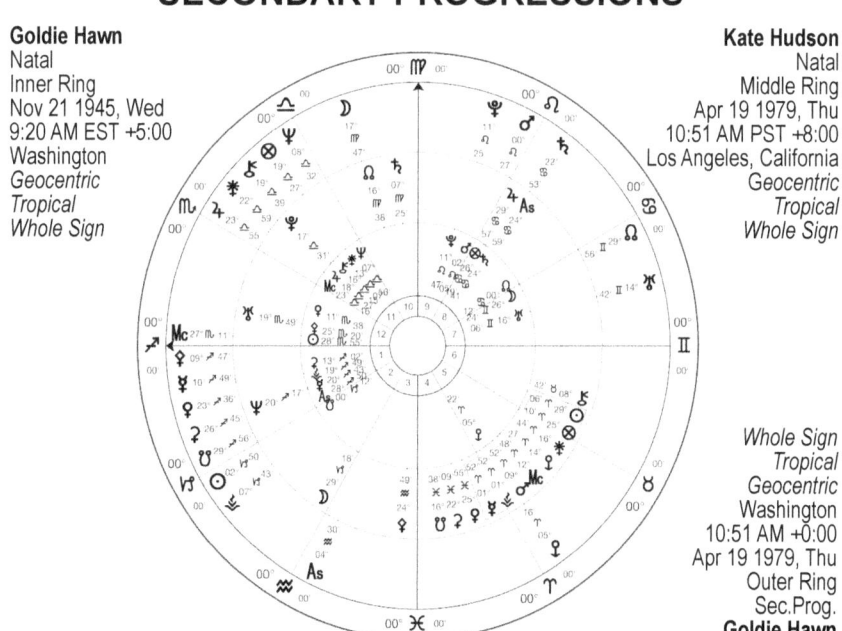

Jaid Barrymore/Drew Barrymore

Jaid and Drew Barrymore's relationship has been one of trial and tribulation. The following chart is for Drew's birth: Feb 22, 1975.

Jaid got Drew into acting at the early age of 11 months. (Jaid's O.P. Mars in Leo opposing Drew's MC)

Drew says her mom treated her more like a best friend than her child. (Jaid's O.P. Juno/O.P. Jupiter square Drew's Moon/Jaid's Saturn) (Jaid's O.P. Moon inconjunct Drew's Juno)

Jaid failed at setting healthy boundaries for Drew. There was no parental support structure or guidance. "I grew up with zero protection and zero consistency"(Jaid's O.P. Ceres inconjunct Jaid's natal Saturn/Drew's Saturn/Moon) (O.P. Moon square Uranus)

Drew accounts in her memoir, Wildflower, that her mom took her to studio 54 instead of school. (Jaid's O.P. Jupiter in a T-square with Drew's Chiron in Aries/10th, and Mars in Capricorn) (Jaid's O.P. Mercury opposing Drews Jupiter, Drew's 9th house)

She exposed Drew to partying and drinking at the age of 9. She committed Drew to an institution, citing emotional problems, at age 13. (Jaid's progressed Sun in a T-square with her O.P. Moon and Drew's natal Neptune in the 6th)

She didn't really know how to be a mother and Drew was emancipated from Jaid's care by the judicial system at the age of 14. (Jaid's O.P. Ceres opposing her natal moon, inconjunct her O.P. Moon and square progressed Sun) (Jaid's O.P. Ceres inconjunct Drew's Moon)

Decades of estrangement ensued due to ongoing conflict. (O.P. Pallas conjunct Drew's Mars opposite Drew's Moon/Jaid's Saturn) (Jaid's O.P. Mars conjunct her natal Moon in Leo)

Although this relationship is complicated to say the least, they are working to heal their relationship and to honor the love that was present as well. (Jaid's O.P. Venus trine Drew's natal Venus)

ORBITAL PROGRESSIONS
Age 28

Jaid Barrymore
Natal Inner Ring
May 8 1946, Wed
10:00 AM CEDT -2:00
Brannenburg,
Germany
*Geocentric
Tropical
Whole Sign*

Drew Barrymore
Natal
Outer Ring
Feb 22 1975, Sat
11:51 AM PST +8:00
Culver City,
California
*Geocentric
Tropical
Whole Sign*

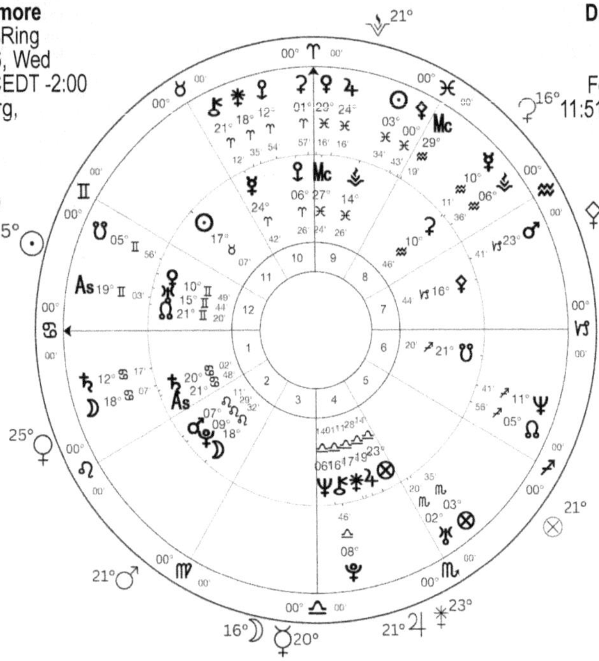

SECONDARY PROGRESSIONS

Jaid Barrymore
Natal Inner Ring
May 8 1946, Wed
10:00 AM CEDT -2:00
Brannenburg,
Germany
*Geocentric
Tropical
Whole Sign*

Drew Barrymore
Natal
Middle Ring
Feb 22 1975, Sat
11:51 AM PST +8:00
Culver City,
California
*Geocentric
Tropical
Whole Sign*

*Whole Sign
Tropical
Geocentric*
Brannenburg,
Germany
11:51 AM CET -1:00
Feb 22 1975, Sat
Outer Ring
Sec.Prog.
Jaid Barrymore

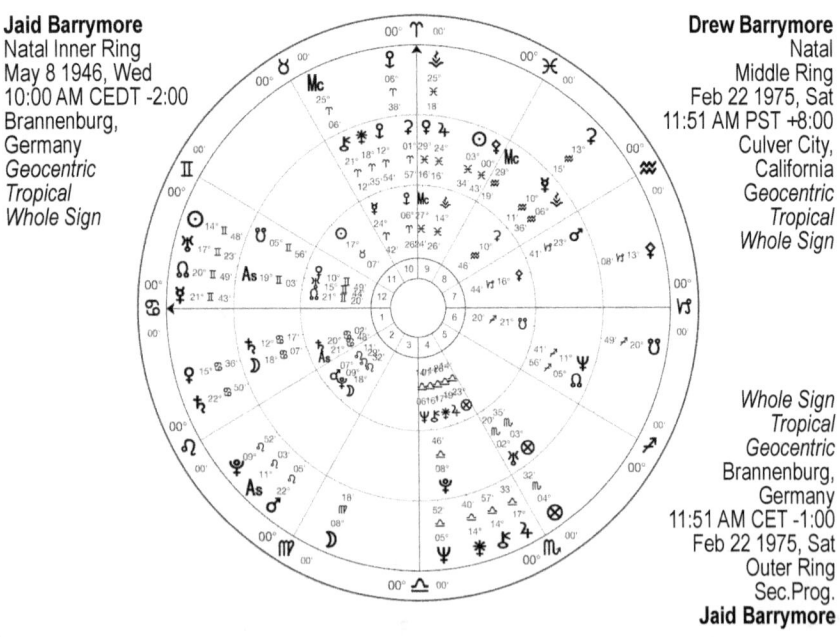

Chapter 7

• • • • • • • •

Bitcoin

Bitcoin

Whether you are a proponent of Bitcoin or not, there's no doubt that crypto currencies, credible crypto currencies, play a huge role in the future economy of the world. Uranus is moving through Taurus at the moment, revolutionary financial changes through technology are upon us. Just as with everything else, when a more logical and efficient system comes along, a shift occurs and evolution happens.

Most people don't send paper letters anymore because we have email. We checkout at the store by tapping our watch on a screen. A digitized currency system is coming up next and there is much to learn. It's rare that a new economic system is created on a planet. Before us lies a fork in the road; one fork leads to more of the old archaic system, the other to a completely new decentralized system, one that empowers everyone instead of the few.

Central Bank Digital Currencies, or CBDCs, are not crypto currencies and that is fundamental to know. Digital currencies are fiat currencies (cash money) that have simply been digitized. They are still completely centralized, meaning they are owned and controlled by the central banking system. There is no transparency.

Crypto currencies are of a completely different nature. We are talking about Bitcoin specifically within this conversation. It is a decentralized network. No one owns it, or you could say everyone who participates in it owns it. There is full transparency.

Blockchain technology stores data on a worldwide ledger for all to see. It's an integrity chain of sorts with many applications even outside of finance. It restores power to the people; fitting for Pluto in Aquarius times.

Bitcoin is the most secure store of wealth that has ever been created. (natal Jupiter in Capricorn trine Saturn) There will only be 21 million ever mined. This is colossal. There is no chance of more just being printed as is done with fiat currencies now.

Even with gold, we know there is more to be mined. With time Bitcoin will only become more and more valuable. The Bitcoin Standard is a great book if you would like to learn more.

People worldwide are liberating themselves from financial tyranny. Governments are beginning to understand the power that Bitcoin possesses. Countries that have weak currencies are now exploring how to create a solid economic infrastructure by adopting Bitcoin as legal tender. A neutral global currency will rebalance and bring integrity to the world's economic landscape.

A new global economic system does not happen overnight, but it does happen. As Pluto moves through Aquarius there will be much more that comes to light. Ultimately, Uranus in Taurus trailed by Pluto in Aquarius, requires us to radically re-evaluate economic sovereignty. It remains to be seen what part Bitcoin will play in all of this.

(Please give me grace on the Bitcoin preach. I have the Sun and Mercury in my 2nd house/Leo so I'm utterly fascinated with this topic.)

We are going to do something a bit different here and look at three different charts. The first chart is for Nov 9, 2021, the day of Bitcoin's highest peak so far.

Bitcoin hit the top of a surprising, euphoric run which took it from $31,000 to $64,000 in a matter of months. (O.P. Venus conjunct O.P. Mercury/natal Uranus/transit Neptune and opposing natal Saturn) (O.P. Venus sextile PoF and progressed Sun)

Saturn and Uranus are in opposition in Bitcoin's natal chart. For Bitcoin, this has equated to rather extreme volatility, much like we see with a volcano when a new island is being formed. Stability comes later in the process. Still, as volatile as it is, long term holders have gained an average of 200% per year.

The next two charts represent potentially interesting times coming up for bitcoin. I will say that the use of Orbital Progressions has allowed me to make a couple of exact, to the day calls on Bitcoin. One was for March 2. 2022 where it had the highest green candle since Oct of the previous year. Price went from $34,322.00 on February 23 to $44,993.12 on March 1, a 56% jump.

By no means am I a financial astrologer. These charts are just to have some fun with and are for your own interpretation. They're definitely not meant for any sort of financial advice. I've noted where the eclipses will be taking place. Depending on when this book is published, we may or may not know what has become of Bitcoin to this point.

ORBITAL PROGRESSIONS
Age 12.5

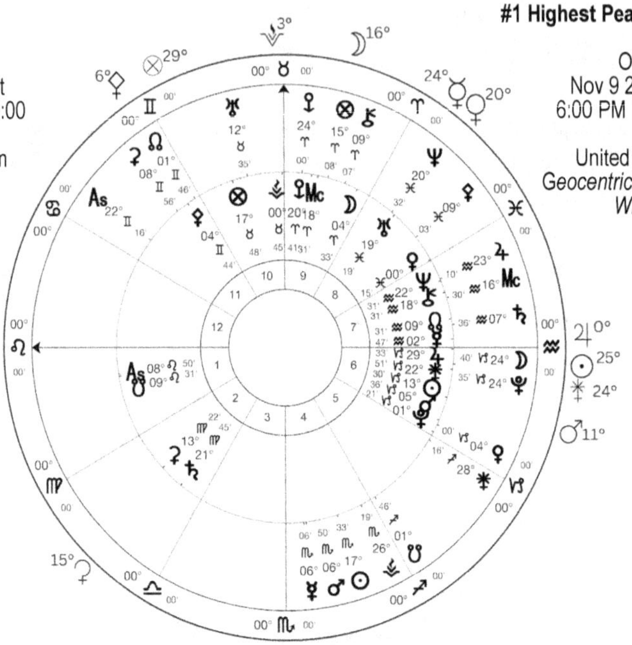

SECONDARY PROGRESSIONS

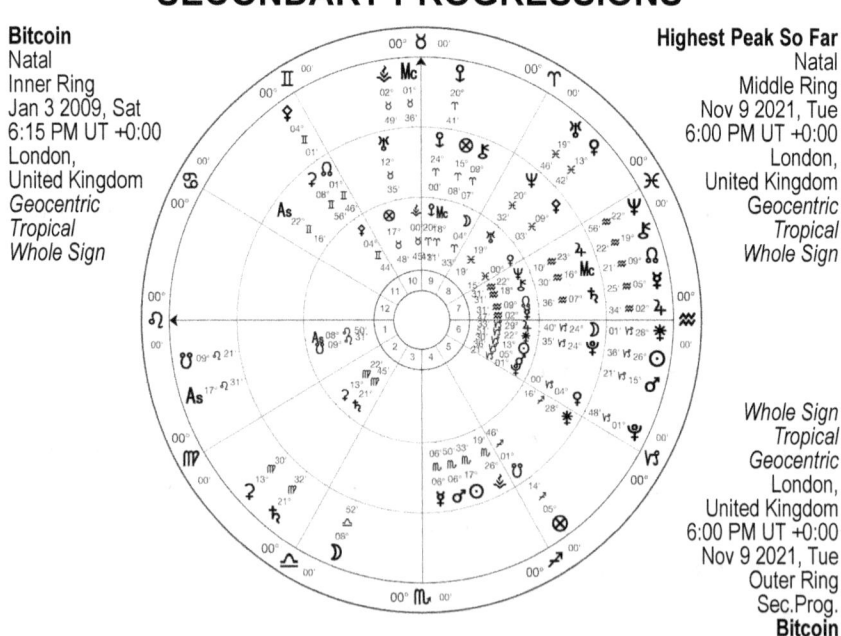

ORBITAL PROGRESSIONS
Age 14

Bitcoin
Natal
Inner Ring
Jan 3 2009, Sat
6:15 PM UT +0:00
London,
United Kingdom
Geocentric
Tropical
Whole Sign

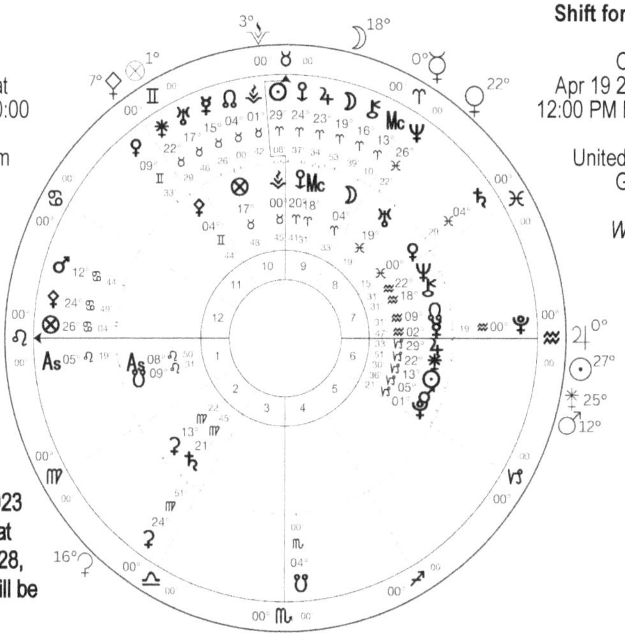

Shift for Bitcoin?
Event
Outer Ring
Apr 19 2023, Wed
12:00 PM BST -1:00
London,
United Kingdom
Geocentric
Tropical
Whole Sign

#2: April 19, 2023 eclipse will be at 29° Aries. Oct 28, 2023 eclipse will be at 5° Taurus.

SECONDARY PROGRESSIONS

Bitcoin
Natal
Inner Ring
Jan 3 2009, Sat
6:15 PM UT +0:00
London,
United Kingdom
Geocentric
Tropical
Whole Sign

Shift for Bitcoin?
Event
Middle Ring
Apr 19 2023, Wed
12:00 PM BST -1:00
London,
United Kingdom
Geocentric
Tropical
Whole Sign

Whole Sign
Tropical
Geocentric
London,
United Kingdom
12:00 PM BST -1:00
Apr 19 2023, Wed
Outer Ring
Sec.Prog.
Bitcoin

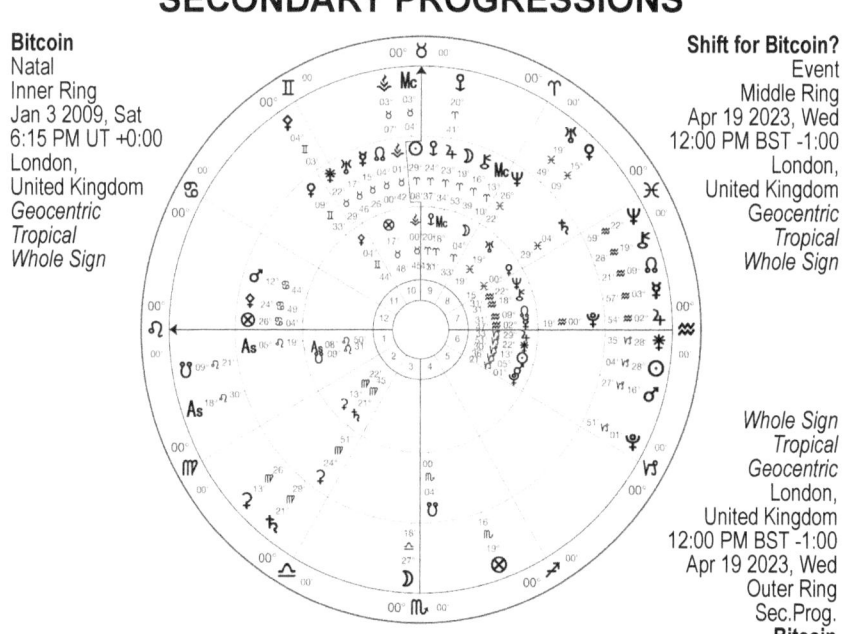

ORBITAL PROGRESSIONS
Age 15

Bitcoin
Natal
Inner Ring
Jan 3 2009, Sat
6:15 PM UT +0:00
London,
United Kingdom
Geocentric
Tropical
Whole Sign

To the Moon?
Natal
Outer Ring
May 22 2024, Wed
12:00 PM BST -1:00
London,
United Kingdom
Geocentric
Tropical
Whole Sign

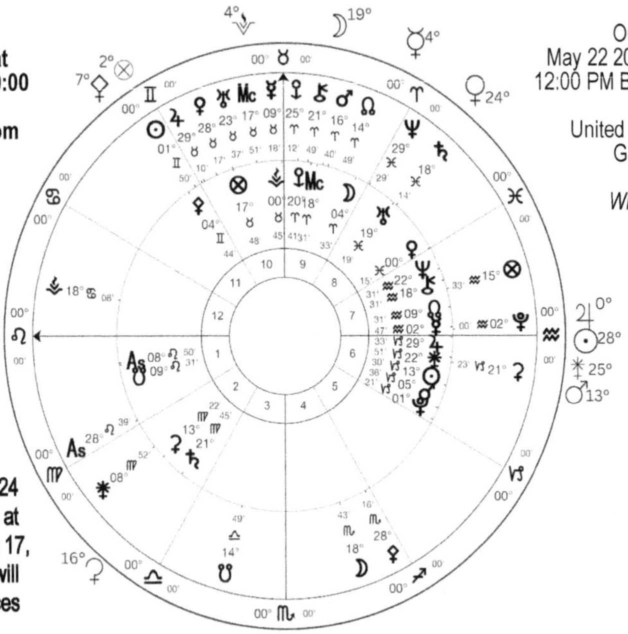

#3: April 8, 2024 eclipse will be at 19° Aries/Sep 17, 2024 eclipse will be at 25° Pisces

SECONDARY PROGRESSIONS

Bitcoin
Natal
Inner Ring
Jan 3 2009, Sat
6:15 PM UT +0:00
London,
United Kingdom
Geocentric
Tropical
Whole Sign

To the Moon?
Natal
Middle Ring
May 22 2024, Wed
12:00 PM BST -1:00
London,
United Kingdom
Geocentric
Tropical
Whole Sign

Whole Sign
Tropical
Geocentric
London,
United Kingdom
12:00 PM BST -1:00
May 22 2024, Wed
Outer Ring
Sec.Prog.
Bitcoin

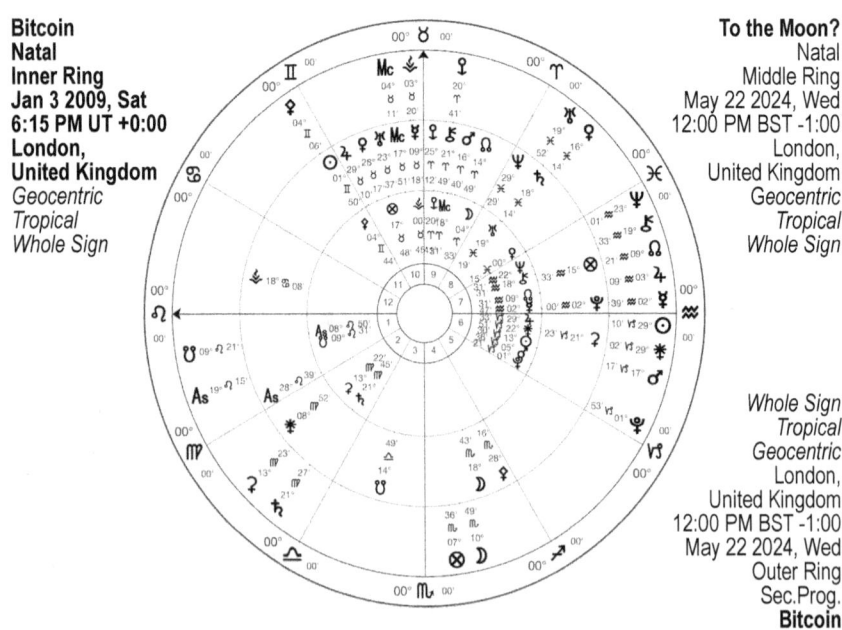

Chapter 8
Come Back Queens of Stranger Things

Kate Bush

I was 10 when Kate Bush's most acclaimed album, Hounds of Love, was released. I remember rolling around to her tunes at the skating rink and catching an occasional video of hers on M.T.V. , which I had to watch at my friend's house because my T.V. at home was a 13 inch turn dial with rabbit ears and no cable…the horror! There was something just as captivating about her then as there is now.

Accolades to her for being the first female artist to have a UK number one self-written song, for being a three-time Grammy nominee, and receiving three nominations for the Rock and Roll Hall of Fame. She's had a strong career as a songstress, with a slew of awards in her wake. For any of you Pink Floyd fans out there, David Gilmore helped her record her first professional demo tape. She was signed with EMI Records at the age of 16.

Sure, she knew "Running Up That Hill" was good; it bumped Madonna's "Like A Virgin" out of the number one chart position in England. But did she, or anyone else for that matter, ever think that 40 years later it would be blowing up the charts, and her bank account decades later? Probably not.

The following chart is for the release of Stranger Things, Season 4 on May 27, 2022.

Boom, her popularity skyrocketed overnight. "Running Up That Hill" has been streamed almost 500 million times worldwide since the airing of Stranger Things.. (O.P. Venus conjunct O.P. Progressed Jupiter, natal Jupiter and North Node in her 11th)

The song is the saving grace for a teenage girl's soul on an American science fiction horror drama television series. (O.P. Jupiter conjunct natal Neptune in Scorpio/12th)

Clearly, large financial gains come with such preeminence. (Grand cross between O.P. Jupiter/natal NN/Neptune, transit Venus/natal SN/Mars, transit Pluto, and transit PoF/O.P. PoF)

It was a media renaissance for her career. (O.P. Mercury conjunct transit Mercury T-squaring natal Pluto/10th, and transit Saturn/3rd) (O.P. Mercury trine Pluto/2nd) The lunar eclipse on Nov. 19, 2021 at 27° Taurus was exactly conjunct O.P. Mercury.

ORBITAL PROGRESSIONS

Age 63.5

Kate Bush
Natal
Inner Ring
Jul 30 1958, Wed
2:30 PM CST +6:00
Bexleyheath
Geocentric
Tropical
Whole Sign

Running Up that Hill 2022
Natal
Outer Ring
May 27 2022, Fri
12:00 PM BST -1:00
Abingdon,
United Kingdom
Geocentric
Tropical
Whole Sign

SECONDARY PROGRESSIONS

Kate Bush
Natal
Inner Ring
Jul 30 1958, Wed
2:30 PM CST +6:00
Bexleyheath
Geocentric
Tropical
Whole Sign

Running Up that Hill 2022
Natal
Middle Ring
May 27 2022, Fri
12:00 PM BST -1:00
Abingdon,
United Kingdom
Geocentric
Tropical
Whole Sign

Whole Sign
Tropical
Geocentric
Bexleyheath
12:00 PM +0:00
May 27 2022, Fri
Outer Ring
Sec.Prog.
Kate Bush

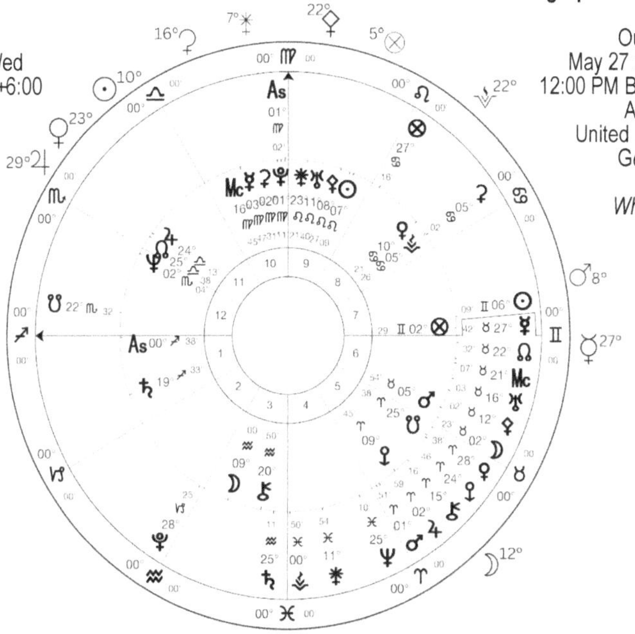

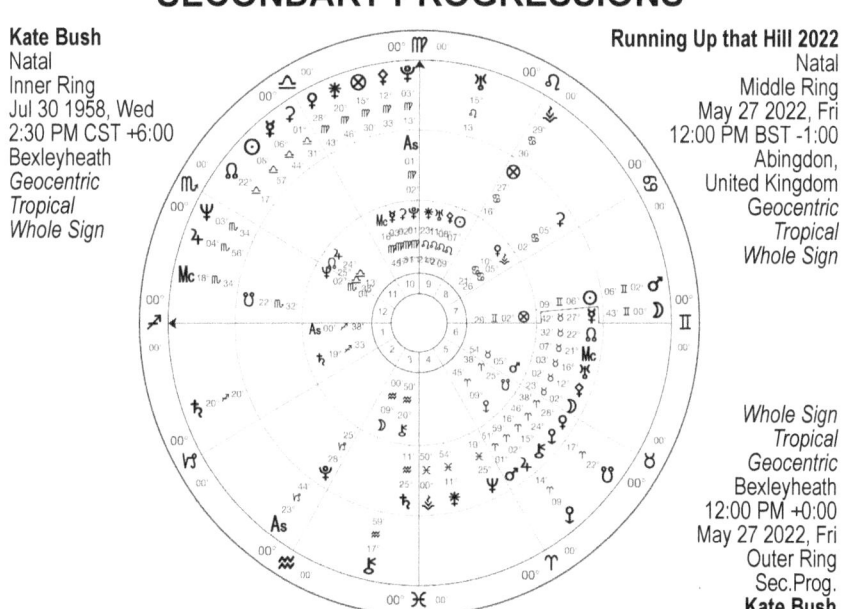

Winona Ryder

Winona Laura Horowitz, a.k.a. Winona Ryder was the chosen ingenue of the late 80"s and 90"s. Although she's cruising through midlife now, she still exudes an endearing innocence that magnetizes her audience and creates a depth of connection; no doubt a lovely byproduct of that 12th house Scorpio Sun/stellium infused with the elixir of her Neptune/Jupiter/Ascendent in Sag.

From Beetlejuice to Stranger Things, Winona has almost 50 movies under her belt, as well as many other notable projects. She's been nominated for two Academy awards, won three Golden Globes, a Grammy, and seven Screen Actors Guild awards. She's had plenty of ups and downs along the way; but, who hasn't right?

With the popularity of Stranger Things she's managed to garner nostalgic adoration from the children of the 80's and respect from the Alpha Gen with one fell swoop.

Here's a fun fact, it turns out she's the one who lobbied to use Kate Bush's song. So Winona is responsible, at least in part, for Running Up That Hill being used in the series.

The following chart is for the release of Stranger Things, Season 1 on July 15, 2016.

Winona has won her way back into our hearts again with her role as quirky, divorced, single mom, Joyce Byers. (Grand trine between O.P. Ceres, O.P. Moon/transit Uranus, and progressed Sun) This is so apropos considering she's playing a mother who battles dark forces and killer Demogorgons from another underworld dimension to retrieve her son; literally portraying the mythology of Ceres.

She's made millions since the release of the first episode. (O.P. Mercury/O.P. PoF in T-square with natal Venus/transit Mars, and natal Mars) (O.P. Venus trine natal Pluto/MC)

The horror series has revived her career. (Grand trine between O.P. Venus/Natal Vesta in 3rd, natal M.C., and natal Saturn in Gemini) (O.P. Venus/NN T-squaring natal Sun in Scorpio, and transit Venus/Mercury/natal SN) (O.P. Jupiter/transit Saturn opposition to O.P. Pallas) (O.P. Mars/SN in a T-square with transit Jupiter/NN, and progressed Sun)

The solar eclipse on March 8, 2016 at 18° 57' Pisces was conjunct O.P. Mars.

ORBITAL PROGRESSIONS

Age 44.5

Winona Ryder
Natal
Inner Ring
Oct 29 1971, Fri
11:00 AM CDT +5:00
Rochester,
Minnesota
Geocentric
Tropical
Whole Sign

Stranger Things
Natal
Outer Ring
Jul 15 2016, Fri
12:00 PM PDT +7:00
Los Angeles,
California
Geocentric
Tropical
Whole Sign

SECONDARY PROGRESSIONS

Winona Ryder
Natal
Inner Ring
Oct 29 1971, Fri
11:00 AM CDT +5:00
Rochester,
Minnesota
Geocentric
Tropical
Whole Sign

Stranger Things
Natal
Middle Ring
Jul 15 2016, Fri
12:00 PM PDT +7:00
Los Angeles,
California
Geocentric
Tropical
Whole Sign

Whole Sign
Tropical
Geocentric
Rochester,
Minnesota
12:00 PM
CDT +5:00
Jul 15 2016, Fri
Outer Ring
Sec.Prog.
Winona Ryder

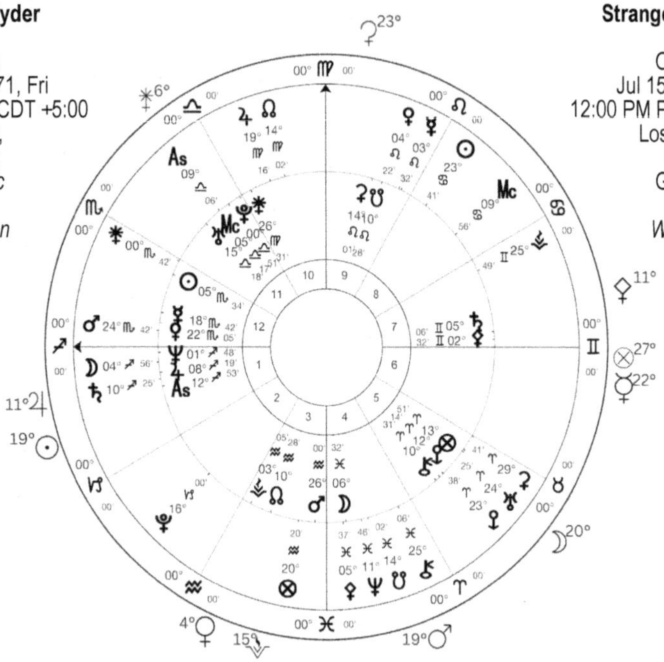

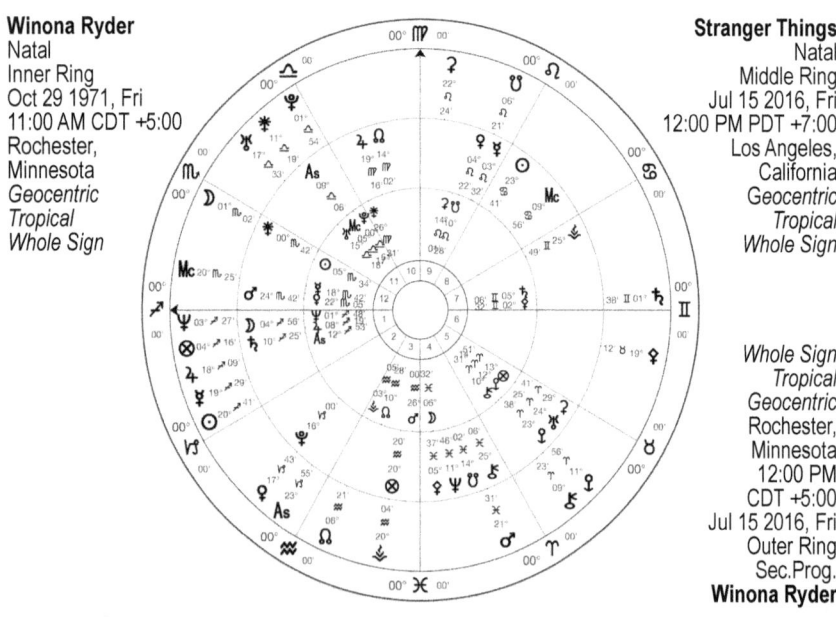

Chapter 9
• • • • • • • •
Musicians

Amy Winehouse

Such a powerful voice radiated from this tiny, tortured songbird. If you've seen the documentary Amy, you see this bright, goofy young girl with the voice of a well-seasoned soul singer who gets swept up in the vortex of fame and the dark side that can come with it.

Her music permeates the soul with its bittersweet yet catchy melodies. No one's ever made rebelling against rehab sound so great. Ultimately rehab is what she needed in order to heal herself but that wasn't in the cards for her, or other members of the 27 club. Could it be that those brilliant artists, from their higher perspective, intended short lives; simply incarnating to reach the zenith of musical mastery, then leave?

The following chart is for the release of Back to Black: Oct 27, 2006.

The album attracted critical acclaim and captured the attention of one of her lifelong idols, the legendary Tony Benett. It won 5

Grammys, went double platinum, and has sold over 16 million copies worldwide. (O.P. Mercury/transit Pluto/natal Neptune trine natal Venus/transit Saturn in Leo/3rd) (O.P. PoF trine natal Jupiter/Uranus in Sagittarius)

Back to Black was the lyrical mourning of the end of her tumultuous relationship with Blake Fielder-Civil, one fueled by passion, obsession and abuse, both physical and drugs. He had been having an affair with Amy but, in a surprise move, he left her to return to his ex. (O.P. Mercury/transit Pluto/natal Neptune/7th in a T-square with O.P. Vesta/transit Juno) (O.P. Jupiter exactly conjunct natal Uranus)

Amy's life had spiraled out of control. She unfortunately was struggling with bulimia at this point in her life as well. (O.P. Mercury/natal Pluto/Moon square natal Mercury in Virgo) (O.P. Ceres square transit Jupiter/Mercury, and inconjunct O.P. Venus/natal Sun/Mercury)

No doubt she was battling her inner demons. (O.P. Pallas in the 8th square progressed Sun)

The lunar eclipse on March 14, 2006 at 24° Virgo was conjunct O.P. Venus and square O.P. Mercury.

ORBITAL PROGRESSIONS
Age 23

Amy Winehouse
Natal
Inner Ring
Sep 14 1983, Wed
10:25 PM BST -1:00
London,
United Kingdom
Geocentric
Tropical
Whole Sign

Back to Black
Natal
Outer Ring
Oct 27 2006, Fri
12:00 PM BST -1:00
London,
United Kingdom
Geocentric
Tropical
Whole Sign

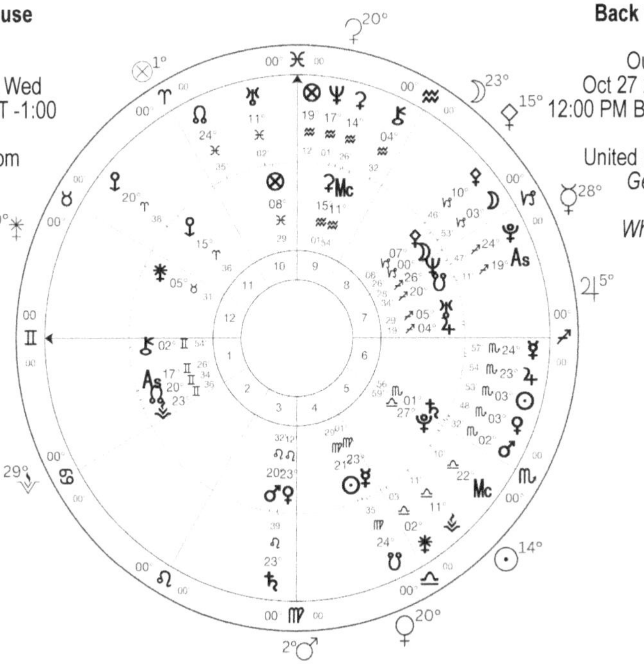

SECONDARY PROGRESSIONS

Amy Winehouse
Natal
Inner Ring
Sep 14 1983, Wed
10:25 PM BST -1:00
London,
United Kingdom
Geocentric
Tropical
Whole Sign

Back to Black
Natal
Middle Ring
Oct 27 2006, Fri
12:00 PM BST -1:00
London,
United Kingdom
Geocentric
Tropical
Whole Sign

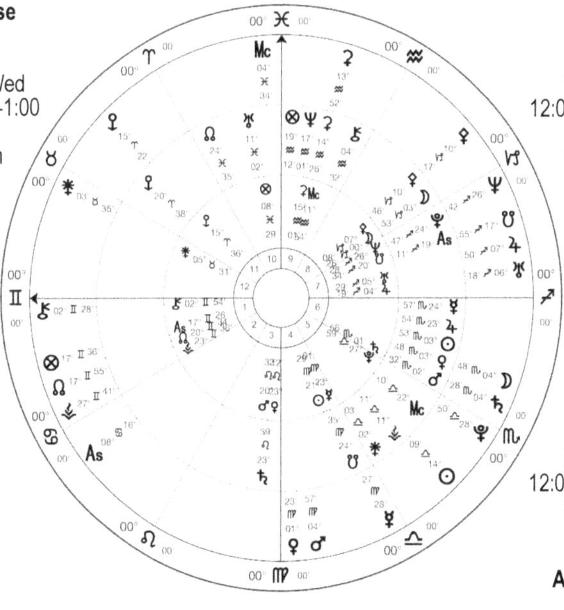

Whole Sign
Tropical
Geocentric
London,
United Kingdom
12:00 PM BST -1:00
Oct 27 2006, Fri
Outer Ring
Sec.Prog.
Amy Winehouse

Prince

"Dearly beloved, we are gathered here today to get through this thing we call life." Amen and hallelujah, Prince. With that packed stellium in his 10th house, Leo, how could this man not take us on a funk-filled, passionate, melodious, odyssey of sexual revolution? And damn, that confidence, I'd like just a spoonful of that please.

Remember the Superbowl halftime show where the network was like don't try any funny business and he literally created a giant silhouette of himself stroking his... guitar?

He was brilliant at expressing the taboo. He wrote and handed out chart toppers like candy to plenty of other musicians of the 80's, like " I Feel for You", Chaka Khan.

Stevie Nicks' "Stand Back" is actually a rewrite of "Little Red Corvette"; Prince, in full support, played synthesizer in her version. He handed out a little deity called "Kiss" but ended up taking it back for himself.

The following chart is for the release of "Kiss", on Feb 5, 1986.

The vibe of this track and video have hilariously been described as "swaggering fuck-squeak" and "some of the greatest peacocking ever put to film."- Tom Breihan, Stereogum. LOL. (O.P. Venus/ O.P Vesta/transiting Pallas/natal Sun in the 8th opposing transit Uranus) This alignment also represents the song skyrocketing to the top of the billboard charts, holding the number one position for weeks.

"Kiss" delivered a Grammy for Best R&B performance by a Duo or Group with Vocals. (O.P. Mercury opposing natal Mars/O.P. Moon)

To this day it continues to gross millions worldwide. (Grand Trine between O.P. Venus/O.P. Vesta, natal Jupiter, and transiting Jupiter/Venus/Mercury/Sun.)

In the same year Kiss was released, Prince directed and acted in a romantic comedy called Under the Cherry Moon, a love story about a con artist who is planning to swindle and heiress only he ends up really falling in love with her. (O.P. Moon in the 5th opposite O.P. Mercury; trine natal Juno) (O.P. Juno inconjunct transit Neptune, square transit Pluto)

The solar eclipse on April 9, 1986 was at 19° Aries conjunct O.P. Mars; fitting for a song so overtly masculine in nature.

ORBITAL PROGRESSIONS
Age 27.5

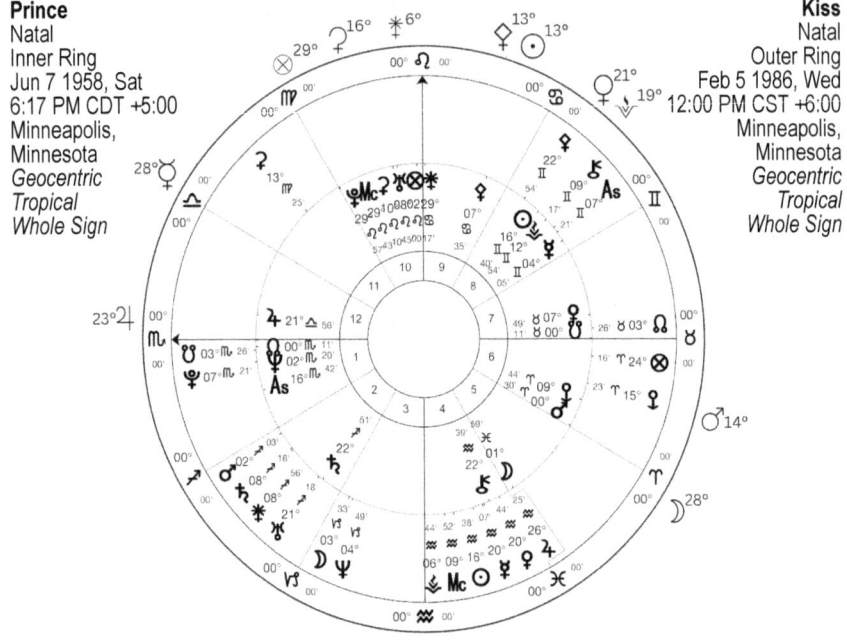

SECONDARY PROGRESSIONS

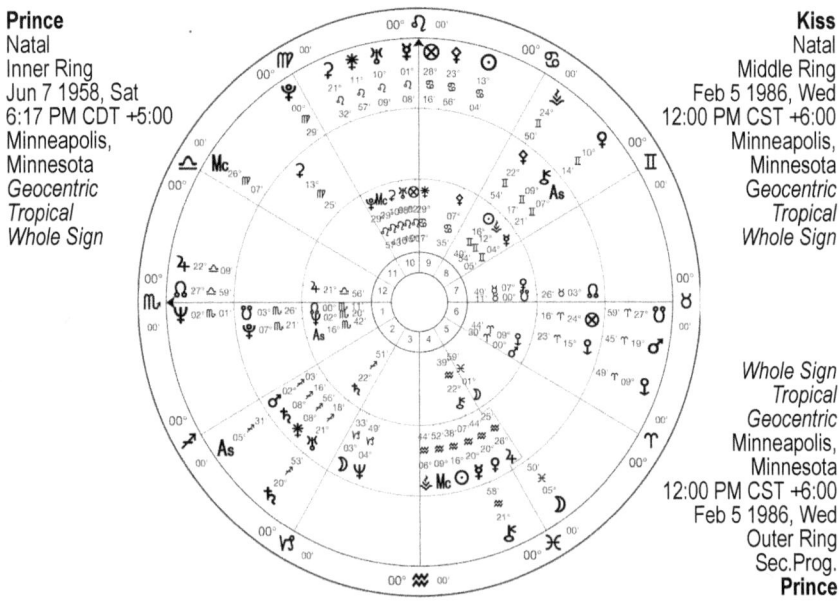

David Bowie

What do you say about The Man who Sold the World on glam rock?

The virtuoso known as David Bowie blew open minds and skyrocketed into fame when he appeared as the extraterrestrial rock star Ziggy Stardust on Top of the Pops in 1972. Bowie WAS otherworldly. Would any of us be surprised to find out he was, in fact, an alien posing as a rock star?

He was this remarkable kaleidoscope of Avant Garde talent, and just fucking cool. Musical maestro...clearly. Rebel Rebel. Young Americans. Fame. Golden Years.

Heroes. We could go on, and on, and on. He took sound in a completely new radical, rebellious direction.

Acclaimed actor...Labyrinth anyone? Jareth was pure beguiling, iconic brilliance.

In reality, his entire life was an odyssey of theatrical expression. He actually trained as a mime before his career took off. There was difficulty in expressing himself as David Jones, but as the ever-changing character, Bowie, he found the freedom to portray his internal dialog.

The following chart is for the release of "Let's Dance" on April 14, 1983.

Even though it was completely outside of his norm, it immediately hit the top of the charts and was his most commercially successful album. (O.P. Mercury opposite transit Jupiter/Uranus; sextile natal Saturn/Pluto)

He dramatically reinvented himself and took on a bold, new, more American style and persona. (Grand trine between O.P. Mercury/5th, natal Neptune/9th, and Ascendent/O.P. Mars/O.P. Pallas) The mainstream loved it but his cult following criticized it. (O.P. Venus square Saturn)

A few months prior he starred in, Merry Christmas Mr. Lawrence. Although it didn't didn't do very well at the box office, he won critical acclaim. (O.P. Mercury/5th opposing transit Uranus/Jupiter/Venus/MC)

Two years earlier he had been awarded sole custody of his son just as O.P. Mercury was crossing into the 5th house, squaring Ceres. He was disciplined and determined to be present for Duncan. (O.P. Mars opposite natal Saturn/Moon in Leo) He was getting sober and working on his mental health after a long stint with cocaine. (Grand trine between O.P. Mars, natal Neptune, and O.P. Mercury)

ORBITAL PROGRESSIONS
Age 36

David Bowie
Natal
Inner Ring
Jan 8 1947, Wed
9:00 AM UT +0:00
London,
United Kingdom
Geocentric
Tropical
Whole Sign

Let's Dance
Natal
Outer Ring
Apr 14 1983, Thu
12:00 PM BST -1:00
London,
United Kingdom
Geocentric
Tropical
Whole Sign

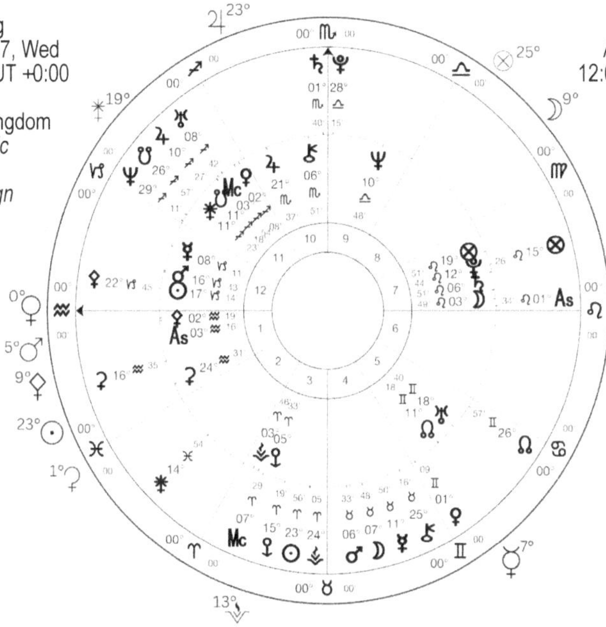

SECONDARY PROGRESSIONS

David Bowie
Natal
Inner Ring
Jan 8 1947, Wed
9:00 AM UT +0:00
London,
United Kingdom
Geocentric
Tropical
Whole Sign

Let's Dance
Natal
Middle Ring
Apr 14 1983, Thu
12:00 PM BST -1:00
London,
United Kingdom
Geocentric
Tropical
Whole Sign

Whole Sign
Tropical
Geocentric
London, United
Kingdom 12:00 PM
BST -1:00
Apr 14 1983, Thu
Outer Ring Sec.Prog.
David Bowie

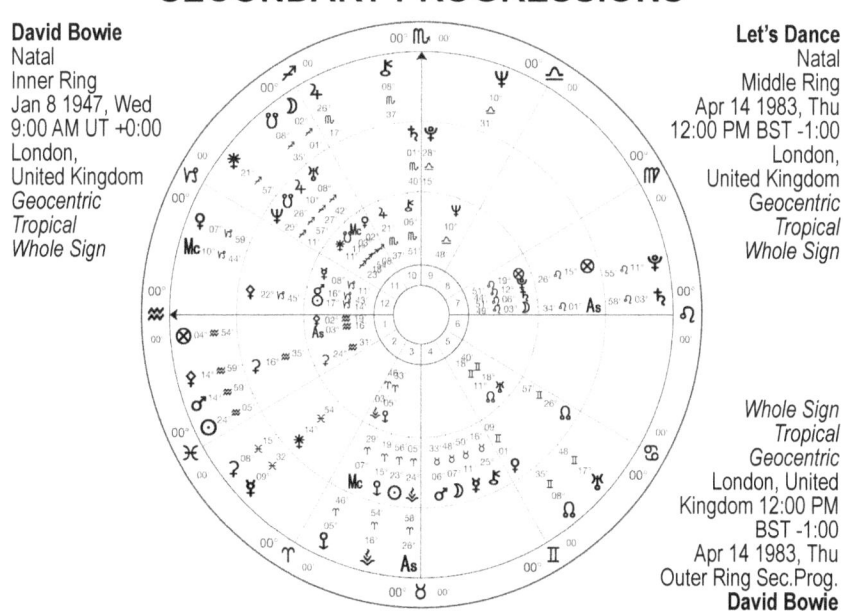

Chapter 10
• • • • • • • • •
Royals

Princess Diana

Diana came to teach on the world's stage. She had a normal life in the beginning. This would prove to be a blessing and a curse, although nothing is really a curse when we understand that we choose everything from a soul perspective. She agreed to show humanity the pitfalls of a monarchy, to model grace and compassion for all beings, and to exhibit courage in the face of adversity.

The following chart is for the wedding of Diana to Prince Charles on July 29, 1981. It was the proverbial fairytale, or so she thought. (O.P. Venus opposing transit Neptune) She very much felt that she had found the partner of her dreams. But time would tell if his love, or lack thereof, was at odds with the love she craved.

Eventually, in a bold move, she would petition for the right to divorce from a loveless marriage. (O.P. Venus square natal Juno/Pallas)

Defined by her title of Princess, she was beloved in the hearts of the people. (Grand trine between O.P. Venus, natal MC/transit Pluto, and natal Moon in Aquarius)

Marriage into the royal family brought with it an unusual, obnoxious, amount of wealth. (O.P. Part of Fortune conjunct Uranus in Leo) (O.P. Moon/natal PoF/transit NN/Pallas/Sun opposing natal Jupiter/SN) (O.P. Venus trine transit Pluot/Juno)

The solar eclipse on July 31. 1981 at 7° Leo, 2 days after their wedding, was conjunct O.P. Moon/progressed Sun. She became pregnant within two months of getting married.

Princess Diana became a fashion icon and trend setter for women around the world, although she wasn't comfortable with being idolized. (O.P. Moon conjunct transit Sun/Pallas in the 9th/Leo) (O.P. Moon square natal Neptune)

She was the obsession of the paparazzi, who relentlessly followed her for photos. (T-square between O.P. Mercury, O.P. Venus, and transit Neptune)

She took the responsibilities of her status seriously and made it her mission to bring attention to humanitarian causes. (O.P. Pallas trine transit Uranus) (O.P. Venus sextile transit Jupiter/Saturn in the 11th/Libra) (O.P. Moon opposite natal Jupiter in Aquarius)

ORBITAL PROGRESSIONS
Age 20

Princess Diana
Natal
Inner Ring
Jul 1 1961, Sat
7:45 PM BST -1:00
Sandringham
Geocentric
Tropical
Whole Sign

Royal Wedding
Natal
Outer Ring
Jul 29 1981, Wed
11:17 AM BST -1:00
London, United Kingdom
Geocentric
Tropical
Whole Sign

SECONDARY PROGRESSIONS

Princess Diana
Natal
Inner Ring
Jul 1 1961, Sat
7:45 PM BST -1:00
Sandringham
Geocentric
Tropical
Whole Sign

Royal Wedding
Natal
Middle Ring
Jul 29 1981, Wed
11:17 AM BST -1:00
London,
United Kingdom
Geocentric
Tropical
Whole Sign

Whole Sign
Tropical
Geocentric
Sandringham
11:17 AM BST -1:00
Jul 29 1981, Wed
Outer Ring
Sec.Prog.
Princess Diana

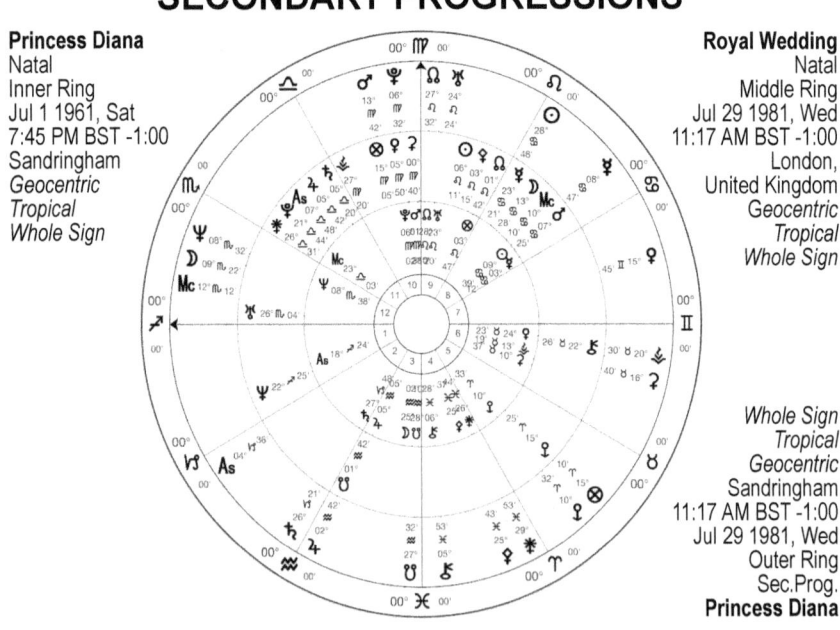

Prince Harry

Since the moment he was born into the monarchy, Harry has been a royal maverick. He's just not wired to go with the imperial flow; a literal, royal pain in the ass. He was forged in the womb of his mother at the time anarchy was starting to smolder in her soul. The imprint of our mother is a powerful thing. It is, of course, up to us how we use it. Harry has chosen to follow in his mother's footsteps, to pull back the curtain and expose more of the ruling family's dark underbelly.

The following chart is for Jan 8. 2020; the day Harry and Meghan made the shocking and unprecedented announcement that they would be splitting from the royal family. At the moment there were no details given as to why, but in time the secrets would emerge. (O.P. Mercury in exact square Pluto in Scorpio, and T-square to Uranus)

How appropriate that O.P. Mercury was poised at 0° Capricorn/1st house right as they announced leaving the monarchy, Capricorn, in order to have a more normal life amongst everyday people, Aquarius?

They stated that they, as a couple, were setting out in order to develop a "progressive new role", and that they would be residing overseas. This burned bridges with the family. (O.P. Venus conjunct natal Uranus/Mars in Sagittarius; T-square to O.P. Pallas/O.P. Vesta; O.P. Mars square transit Chiron in the 4th)

He was choosing his wife over the Queen. (O.P. Venus opposing transit Moon)

Here's a shocker, turns out the monarchy is racist. Who would have thought? Can we assume everyone in it is? No, but the cancer that is racism runs deep in their blood. While the majority of comments about finally having a blended royal family are very positive (O.P. Mercury trine O.P.Ceres), there have unfortunately been racist slurs and even death threats towards Harry and Meghan's family. (O.P. Mars opposing O.P. Ceres)

Come to find out, a large part of Harry's motivation in leaving was to keep his beloved nuclear family safe and in a more socially accepting environment than the palace provides. (progressed Sun in grand trine with O.P. Moon/ transit Venus in Aquarius)

The lunar eclipse on June 5, 2020 was at 15° Sagittarius conjunct O.P. Venus.

ORBITAL PROGRESSIONS

Age 35

Prince Harry
Natal
Inner Ring
Sep 15 1984, Sat
4:20 PM BST -1:00
Paddington
Geocentric
Tropical
Whole Sign

Royal Exit
Natal
Outer Ring
Jan 8 2020, Wed
12:00 PM UT +0:00
London,
United Kingdom
Geocentric
Tropical
Whole Sign

SECONDARY PROGRESSIONS

Prince Harry
Natal
Inner Ring
Sep 15 1984, Sat
4:20 PM BST -1:00
Paddington
Geocentric
Tropical
Whole Sign

Royal Exit
Natal
Middle Ring
Jan 8 2020, Wed
12:00 PM UT +0:00
London,
United Kingdom
Geocentric
Tropical
Whole Sign

Whole Sign
Tropical
Geocentric
Paddington
12:00 PM UT +0:00
Jan 8 2020, Wed
Outer Ring
Sec.Prog.
Prince Harry

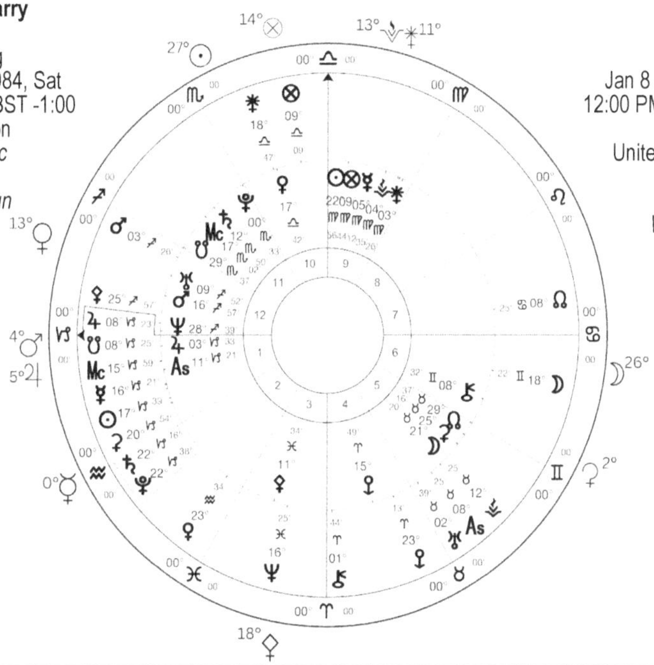

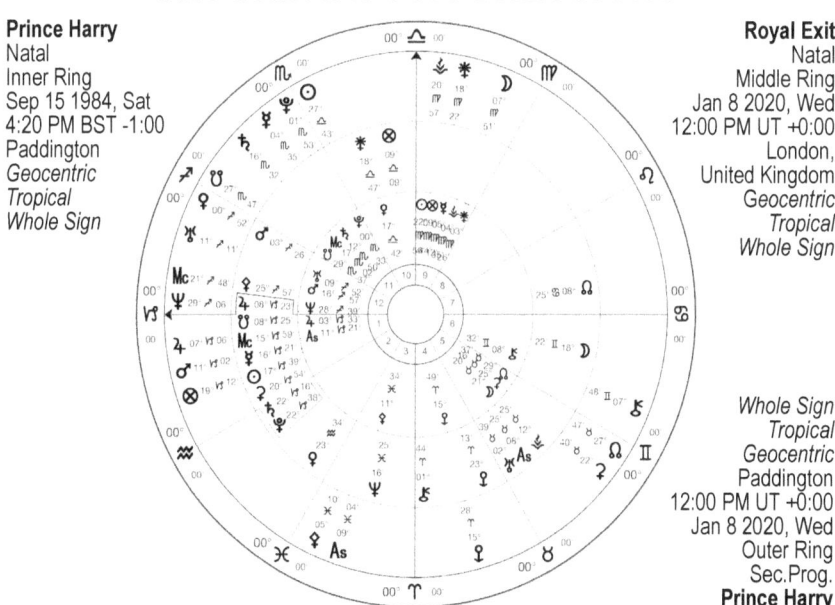

Chapter 11
• • • • • • • • •
Saints

Mother Teresa

Anjezë Gonxhe Bojaxhiu became a nun at 18 and chose the name, Teresa. It means, "to do small things with great love", a creed she strived to live by. Although not perfect (who is?) Mother Teresa genuinely sought to alleviate suffering in the world to the best of her ability. Her efforts have made a profound impact on the psyche of humanity, inspiring care and compassion for all.

The following chart is for the day Mother Teresa received the Nobel Peace Prize, Oct 18, 1979.

It is awarded to her for a lifetime of service and devotion to the needs of the sick and the poor. In a press release, the Norwegian Nobel Committee stated, "This year the world has turned its attention to the plight of children and refugees, and these are precisely the categories for whom Mother Teresa has for many years worked so selflessly"-Nobelprize.org. (O.P. Ceres/O.P. Saturn in the 6th, trine transit Jupiter in Virgo/10th) (O.P. Pallas trine transit Uranus/Mercury in the 12th)

As a Catholic, she spoke out against women's reproductive rights and abortion in her acceptance speech. (O.P. Venus in exact opposition to O.P. Vesta) (O.P. Mercury square O.P. Mars/natal Pluto)

There was some criticism of her at the time, too. She and her charities were based in India. She saw converting Hindus to Christianity as part of her mission. (O.P. Mars/O.P. Jupiter square natal Neptune)

In letters released after her death, she revealed that in 1979 she was having a serious crisis of faith and that she felt like a hypocrite. (O.P. Mars/Jupiter conjunct Pluto in the 11th, square O.P. Mercury in the 8th) (O.P. Pallas square transit Neptune) (O.P. Saturn square natal Venus in the 9th)

She was criticized for her query. But how could she have seen as much horrendous suffering as she did, and not question the powers that be? Perhaps it speaks even more highly of her character that she was questioning her beliefs and re-examining her values. (Grand cross between O.P. Venus at 0°/1st, O.P. Vesta, natal Sun/10th, and natal Chiron/Pallas)

The Lunar eclipse on Sept. 6, 1979 was at 13° Pisces conjunct O.P. Pallas.

ORBITAL PROGRESSIONS
Age 69 (Saturn is used)

Mother Teresa
Natal
Inner Ring
Aug 26 1910, Fri
2:25 PM CET -1:00
Skopje,
Macedonia
*Geocentric
Tropical
Whole Sign*

Nobel Peace Prize
Natal
Middle Ring
Oct 18 1979, Thu
12:00 PM CET -1:00
Oslo, Norway
*Geocentric
Tropical
Whole Sign*

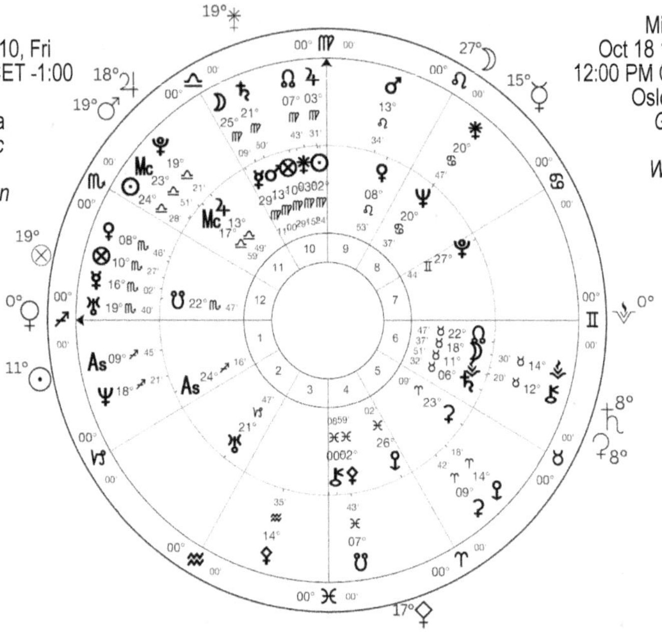

SECONDARY PROGRESSIONS

Mother Teresa
Natal
Inner Ring
Aug 26 1910, Fri
2:25 PM CET -1:00
Skopje, Macedonia
*Geocentric
Tropical
Whole Sign*

Nobel Peace Prize
Natal
Middle Ring
Oct 18 1979, Thu
12:00 PM CET -1:00
Oslo, Norway
*Geocentric
Tropical
Whole Sign*

*Whole Sign
Tropical
Geocentric*
Skopje,
Macedonia
12:00 PM CET -1:00
Oct 18 1979, Thu
Outer Ring
Sec.Prog.
Mother Teresa

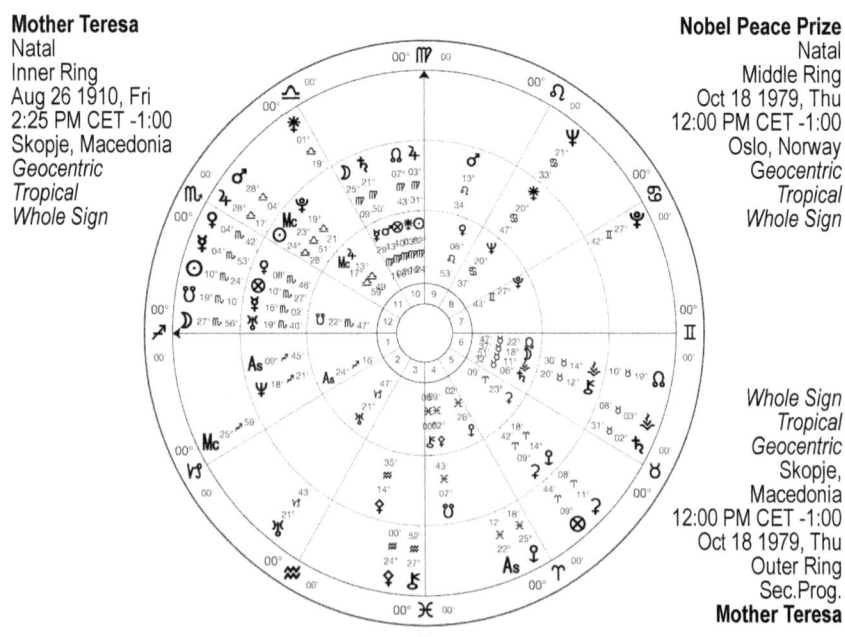

Mr. Rogers

He may not have been canonized but if you want to see the chart of an angel, here it is. Fred Rogers was put here on this Earth to imbue unconditional love and compassion into every child that crossed his path, whether in person or through his show. Just look at that beautiful 11th house stellium in Pisces.

The following chart is for the day he addressed the Senate, May 1, 1969.

If you haven't seen the footage, it's worth a watch. Mr. Rogers had such a peaceful and loving frequency that even the most staunch Senator turned to mush upon listening to him speak. He was fully embracing the role of spiritual warrior as he fought the defunding of children's programming. (O.P. Mars conjunct natal Venus in Pisces) (O.P. Jupiter/12th trine natal Saturn/transit Mars in the 8th)

In his speech he discusses mental health and addresses the importance of programs that teach emotional awareness to children. (O.P. Moon in the 12th/Aries trine O.P. Mercury in the 4th/Leo)

Mr. Rogers sits in front of a rather put-out-looking subcommittee chairman and begins by speaking of the importance of trust. He then proceeds to discuss, in his poised and gentle tone, the importance of learning how to deal with anger and inner conflict, something everyone needed help with as this took place at the time of the Vietnam war. There's a feeling that he's speaking about more than T.V. He's truly speaking to the inner child of each person in that room and they can feel it. (O.P. Venus/Sun in the 1st, sextile O.P. Mars in the 11th/Pisces) (O.P. Moon/O.P. Jupiter trine natal Saturn/8th)

You could hear a pin drop in the room as he began to recite, *"What do you do with the mad that you feel? When you feel so mad you could bite. When the whole wide world seems oh so wrong, and nothing you do seems very right..."*. To that, the senator responded, "Looks like you've just earned the 20 million dollars". And just like that PBS acquired the funding it needed to keep going thanks to Mr. Rogers. (O.P. Jupiter trine natal Saturn/transit Mars in the 8th) (O.P. Jupiter/Moon square Pluto/3rd) (O.P. PoF, in Gemini, trine O.P. Pallas/transit Ceres in 10th, sextile transit Venus, and sextile natal Jupiter)

The lunar eclipse on Aug 27, 1969 at 4° Pisces was conjunct O.P. Mars.

ORBITAL PROGRESSIONS

Age 41

Fred Rogers
Natal
Inner Ring
Mar 20 1928, Tue
8:20 AM EST +5:00
Latrobe,
Pennsylvania
Geocentric
Tropical
Whole Sign

PBS Hearing
Natal
Outer Ring
May 1 1969, Thu
12:00 PM CDT +5:00
Washington
Geocentric
Tropical
Whole Sign

SECONDARY PROGRESSIONS

Fred Rogers
Natal
Inner Ring
Mar 20 1928, Tue
8:20 AM EST +5:00
Latrobe,
Pennsylvania
Geocentric
Tropical
Whole Sign

PBS Hearing
Natal
Middle Ring
May 1 1969, Thu
12:00 PM CDT +5:00
Washington
Geocentric
Tropical
Whole Sign

Whole Sign
Tropical
Geocentric
Latrobe,
Pennsylvania
12:00 PM EDT +4:00
May 1 1969, Thu
Outer Ring
Sec.Prog.
Fred Rogers

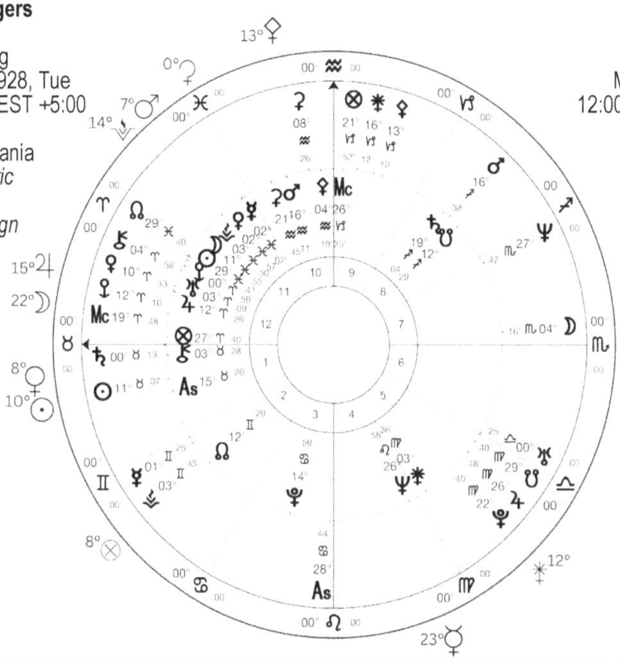

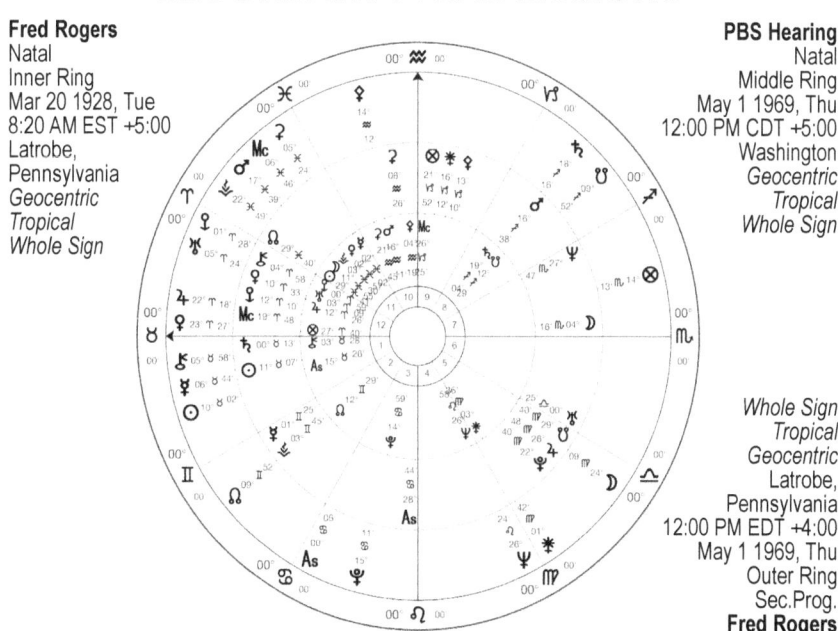

Chapter 12
• • • • • • • • •
Sage & Scientist

Deepak Chopra

Dr. Deepak Chopra has been a wayshower on the leading edge of mind-body wellbeing for over 30 years. He's an endocrinologist turned integrative medicine pioneer, holistic health guru, world renowned speaker, and humanitarian. He's authored over 90 books, 21 of them New York Times Best Sellers, and ushered the ancient science of Ayurveda into a renaissance. Long story short, his teachings are offered as a tool for raising individual/collective consciousness, and, in my opinion, are incredibly valuable if you are seeking to attain self-mastery in life.

I remember the first time I listened to him. I was 19, pregnant, and very focused on becoming more self aware. I scooped up a set of his cassette tapes at a garage sale, "The Higher Self; The Magic of Inner and Outer Fulfillment". From the moment I heard Deepak so brilliantly weaving the levels of existence together, combining scientific data with esoteric wisdom, I was hooked. Seventeen years later I actually ended up going through his Perfect Health certification for Ayurveda, which is a sister science to astrology(Jyotish).

The following is the chart for his first TV appearance on Oprah: July 12, 1993.

The broadcast launched him into fame and significantly elevated his career. (O.P. Mars/10th trine natal Saturn/6th) (O.P. Pallas in Capricorn conjunct transit Pluto/Neptune) (O.P. PoF trine natal Saturn in Leo)

That same year he had just published Ageless Body Timeless Mind, which sold 400,000 copies by the end of its 1st week. The success of this book was a gateway to the Oprah Show. (O.P. Mercury/Gemini opposing natal Venus/Mercury) (O.P. Mercury trine transit Jupiter) (O.P. Moon trine Asc/transiting Pallas/Vesta.) (O.P. PoF trine natal Venus)

The content of the show focused on sacred Ayurvedic principles that help maintain health and beauty while fostering greater self awareness and psychological mastery of the body. (O.P. Mars in Sagittarius exact trine to natal Pluto) (O.P. Venus is opposing natal Pluto in the 12th/6th house, mind/body houses) (O.P. Vesta trine Venus)

The solar eclipse on May 21, 1993 at 0° Gemini was conjunct O.P. Mercury.

The lunar eclipse on June 4, 1993 at 13° Sagittarius was exactly conjunct O.P. Mars.

ORBITAL PROGRESSIONS

Age 46.5

Deepak Chopra
Natal
Inner Ring
Oct 22 1946, Tue
3:45 PM IST -5:30
Delhi, India
Geocentric
Tropical
Whole Sign

Oprah Winfrey Show
Natal Outer Ring
Jul 12 1993, Mon
12:00 PM CDT +5:00
Chicago, Illinois
Geocentric
Tropical
Whole Sign

SECONDARY PROGRESSIONS

Deepak Chopra
Natal
Inner Ring
Oct 22 1946, Tue
3:45 PM IST -5:30
Delhi, India
Geocentric
Tropical
Whole Sign

Oprah Winfrey Show
Natal
Middle Ring
Jul 12 1993, Mon
12:00 PM CDT +5:00
Chicago, Illinois
Geocentric
Tropical
Whole Sign

Whole Sign
Tropical
Geocentric
Delhi, India
12:00 PM IST -5:30
Jul 12 1993, Mon
Outer Ring
Sec.Prog.
Deepak Chopra

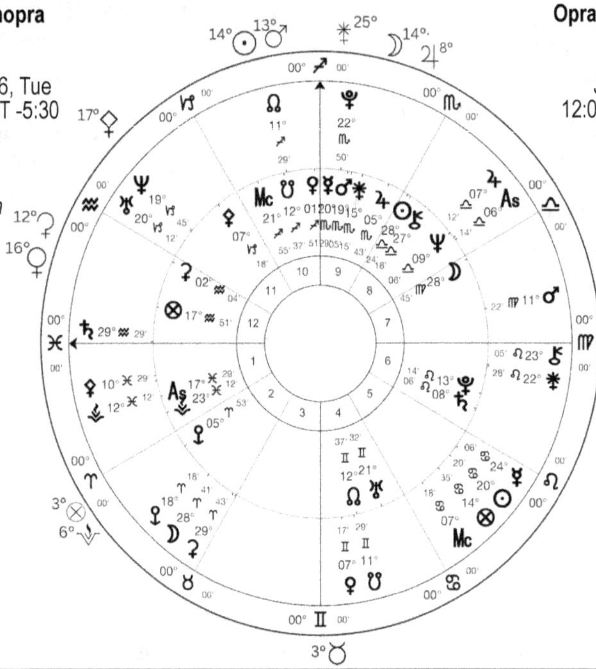

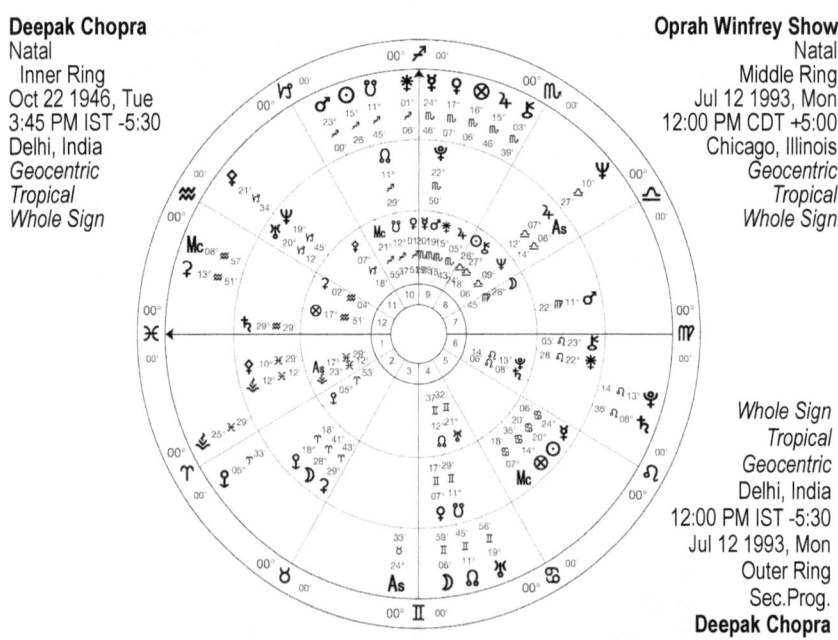

Albert Einstein

Einstein undoubtedly is one of the most influential people of all time. His name is synonymous with genius.

The chart that follows is for the day Einstein submitted the definitive version of his findings in a paper titled, "The Field Equations of Gravitation", aka the 'Theory of Relativity" to the Prussian Academy of Science on Nov 25,1915.

What would we expect to see in the chart of a theoretical physicist at the moment he defines a theory that would change our understanding of the interplay of gravity within space/time? It was profound knowledge which would transform theoretical physics and astronomy forever. (O.P. Mercury conjunct natal Uranus in the 3rd opposing O.P. Jupiter at 29°Aquarius/ 8th) (O.P. Mars conjunct transit Uranus/NNin Aquarius/8th, trine O.P. Venus in Gemini)

The publishing of this paper was the culmination of years of study and research in order to bring forth a completely new concept to the world of science. (O.P. Moon in Capricorn opposing transit Saturn/O.P. Vesta, trining transit Jupiter/Pallas)

This information, as potent as it was, did not win a Nobel Prize. Anti-Semitism was gaining momentum and could have been a factor; Einstein was a Jewish pacifist denouncing WW1 at the time. (O.P. Venus in Gemini/12th square transit Chiron/natal MC in Pisces/9th) (O.P. Mercury inconjunct natal Mercury/Saturn in the 10th)

At this time, in his personal life, he was married to his first wife, Maliva Maric. She was a brilliant physicist in her own right.

They connected through science but they would both admit the marriage lacked romantic love. In 1915, Einstein was having an affair with his cousin and he had just asked Maliva for a divorce, prompting her to move back to Switzerland with the children. (O.P. Venus in Gemini/12th square Chiron in Pisces, trine O.P. Mars/transit Uranus in the 8th, opposing Natal Moon in Sagittarius/6th) (O.P Ceres conjunct natal Pluto, square Jupiter in the 8th) (O.P. Moon/7th in a T-square with transit Saturn/O.P. Vesta and natal Venus/Juno/O.P. Pallas)

The eclipse on Aug 24,1915 was at 0°Pisces, conjunct O.P. Jupiter exactly opposite

O.P. Mercury. Interestingly, an eclipse was used to prove the theory of relativity years later.

ORBITAL PROGRESSIONS

Age 187

Albert Einstein
Male
Inner Ring
Mar 14 1879, Fri
11:30 AM -0:40
Ulm, Germany
Geocentric
Tropical
Whole Sign

Theory of Relativity
Natal
Outer Ring
Nov 25 1915, Thu
12:00 PM CET -1:00
Berlin, Germany
Geocentric
Tropical
Whole Sign

SECONDARY PROGRESSIONS

Albert Einstein
Male Inner Ring
Mar 14 1879, Fri
11:30 AM -0:40
Ulm, Germany
Geocentric
Tropical
Whole Sign

Theory of Relativity
Natal
Middle Ring
Nov 25 1915, Thu
12:00 PM CET -1:00
Berlin, Germany
Geocentric
Tropical
Whole Sign

Whole Sign
Tropical
Geocentric
Ulm, Germany
12:00 PM CET -1:00
Nov 25 1915, Thu
Outer Ring
Sec.Prog.
Albert Einstein

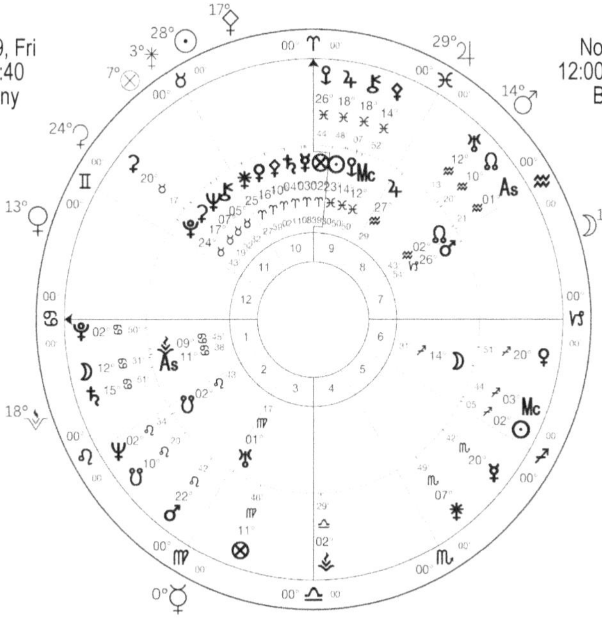

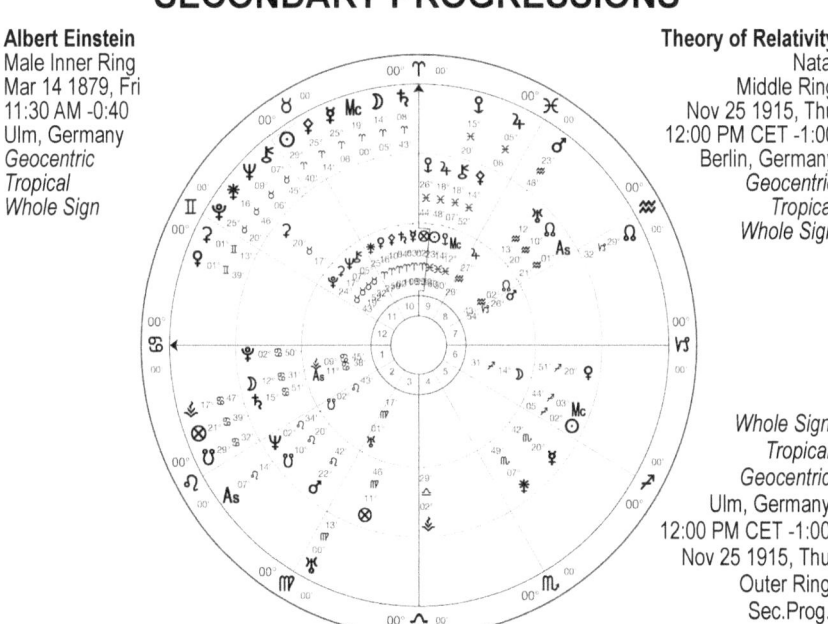

Chapter 13
• • • • • • • • •
The USA

United States of America 1963

Cultural change was in overdrive, and 1963 would prove to be a moment of crisis for America.

The following chart is for the day of the "I Have a Dream" speech on Aug 28, 1963.

Martin Luther King, Jr. eloquently delivers his dream of peace and equality for all people. (O.P. Moon conjunct transit Venus/Sun/Uranus trine O.P. Venus; sextile natal Venus/Jupiter) (O.P. Mercury/natal Neptune trine progressed sun)

He dynamically calls America to action, to right the many wrongs that had been (and continue to be) experienced by African Americans, and to pay back the debt that was promised but not delivered upon. (O.P. Mercury conjunct natal Neptune/transit Pallas square natal Mars in Gemini) (O.P. Venus in the 6th square O.P. PoF/SN in Aquarius)

The speech transpired at the powerful March on Washington for Jobs and Freedom, protesting racial inequality and the lack of social justice. (O.P. Mars at 0° Libra/11th conjunct transit Mercury/natal MC, trine Natal Pluto) Less than a year later the Civil Rights Act would be put into place.

At the same time in America, women, too, were over not being treated as an equal. The Women's Equal Pay Act was signed by John F. Kennedy to prevent discrimination in the workplace due to gender. Until this was signed women were only making 60% of what men were on average for equal work; insert eye roll. (O.P. Moon in the 10th conjunct transit Venus/Sun/Uranus, trine O.P. Venus in the 6th: O.P. Mercury conjunct natal Neptune/transit Pallas trine progressed Sun)

This same year, JFK was assassinated in Dallas, TX. The lunar eclipse on January 19, 1963 at 19° Cancer was exactly conjunct O.P. Jupiter. (Grand cross between O.P. Jupiter/natal Mercury/Sun in the 8th, progressed Sun, O.P. Ceres/transit Jupiter/natal Chiron, and O.P. Saturn/transit Mars/natal Saturn)

The horror of the Vietnam War was festering and anti-war sentiment was starting to set in. (O.P. Saturn in Libra/11th in a T-square with O.P. Jupiter and natal Chiron/transit Jupiter/O.P. Ceres in Aries)

ORBITAL PROGRESSIONS

Age 187

USA (Sibly)
Natal
Inner Ring
Jul 4 1776, Thu
5:10 PM LMT +5:00:39
Philadelphia
Geocentric
Tropical
Whole Sign

1963 (I Have A Dream)
Event
Outer Ring
Aug 28 1963, Wed
5:38:34 PM CST +6:00
Washington
Geocentric
Tropical
Whole Sign

SECONDARY PROGRESSIONS

USA (Sibly)
Natal
Inner Ring
Jul 4 1776, Thu
5:10 PM LMT +5:00:39
Philadelphia
Geocentric
Tropical
Whole Sign

1963 (I Have A Dream)
Event
Middle Ring
Aug 28 1963, Wed
5:38:34 PM CST +6:00
Washington
Geocentric
Tropical
Whole Sign

Whole Sign
Tropical
Geocentric
Philadelphia
5:38 PM EDT +4:00
Aug 28 1963, Wed
Outer Ring
Sec.Prog.
USA (Sibly)

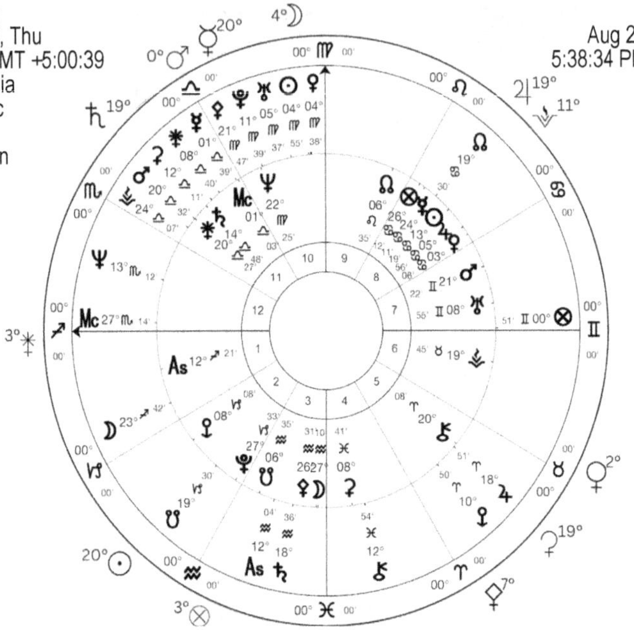

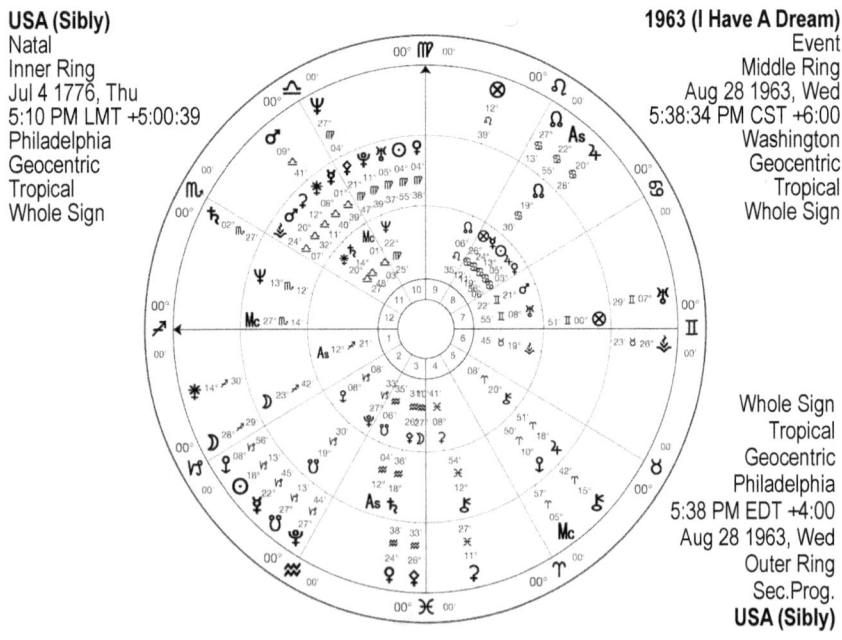

Epilogue

The list could go on and on…

In the creation of this book, there was no cherry picking of charts. Because of the accuracy of this method, it applies to every chart. At this point I've looked at hundreds. It was simply a matter of deciding which one's to include.

If you are an astrologer who hasn't used progressions very much, perhaps this book has made a strong case for using them. When we don't use progressions, we miss out on valuable information.

Have you ever looked at a chart with the natal and transiting planets only, and not been able to find a correlation between an event and that chart? Seemingly, the event is happening in an "empty" space. This happens because we can't see that a progressed planet is actually at that very spot. When we overlay progressions, we fill in blind spots and bring more depth to charts.

Clearly, progressions are an important piece in making accurate predictions. If we don't know where that moving target is, then how can we know when another planet is going to make an aspect to it? We need clarity and precision to make predictions.

If you are an astrologer with years of experience with Secondary Progressions, hopefully Orbital Progressions have managed to pique your curiosity and gain your respect. It's not very often that new information of this nature appears in astrology. After all, Secondary Progressions were discovered over 350 years ago. It's surprising that a twin technique was lying in wait for all these years, but that seems to be the case with these "true" vs "mean" methods.

The validity of this method has been demonstrated throughout this book as we have seen Orbitally Progressed planets align perfectly with natal/transit planets, events, and eclipses. Once you start to play with Orbital Progressions in your chart or readings, it should be further evidence in your own mind that this timing technique delivers reliable and relatable data which will deepen your understanding of the charts that cross your path.

One more thing before we part; I'm not here to be the be all and end all of Orbital progressions. I'm simply offering it as a new method and asking, "What are we going to do with this?".

Who knows the ways in which it may evolve and grow in the future.

I look forward to the many conversations that will arise as we come to more realizations about it.

Thank you for your time and interest as we've explored together.

MERCY JOY MORALES

Astrologer…

Mother. Grandmother. Meditator. Yogini. Ayurveda Enthusiast.

Curious Traveler of Time & Space.

Mercy has had a lifelong fascination with the concept of well-being. Having a mother who preached nutrition and a father who worked in physics, she was inspired to study human existence: why and how we are creating in this reality, what causes harmony and dis-harmony, etc. Metaphysics have been a point of interest since she was a child. These studies have been an integral part of her journey on planet Earth.

The study and practice of astrology has been an ongoing passion of hers for over a decade. Crisis in her life led to a deep dive into this ancient science. She experienced a profound shift as she began to understand life as a series of phases; psychological, emotional, and physical, no different than the seasons. WTF moments have a way of bringing people to astrology but the clarity and insight they discover intrigues them to stay much longer. Time and time again she has witnessed client's fascination as they connect the dots of their lives with the planetary transits that coincide.

Mercy considers herself to be a wholistic astrologer, a bit of a mutt really, pulling wisdom from many different lineages. She's devoted to helping others deepen their self-awareness through the lens of Astrology and loves working with individuals, couples, or families as they explore fundamental energies and the cycles of life. Although Austin, TX is her home, she enjoys working with clients from anywhere in the world via Zoom.

To Connect: mercy@mercyjoyastrology.com

www.ingramcontent.com/pod-product-compliance
Lightning Source LLC
LaVergne TN
LVHW010550070526
838199LV00063BA/4934